Hooked

A Crocheter's Stash of
Wit and Wisdom

Edited by Kari Cornell

Voyageur Press

First published in 2006 by Voyageur Press, an imprint
of MBI Publishing Company, Galtier Plaza, Suite 200,
380 Jackson Street, St. Paul, MN 55101-3885 USA

MBI Publishing Company titles are also available at discounts
in bulk quantity for industrial or sales-promotional use.
For details write to Special Sales Manager at MBI Publishing
Company, Galtier Plaza, Suite 200, 380 Jackson Street,
St. Paul, MN 55101-3885 USA

Library of Congress Cataloging-in-Publication Data

Hooked : a crocheter's stash of wit and wisdom / edited by
Kari Cornell.

    p. cm.
  ISBN-13: 978-0-7603-2647-3
  ISBN-10: 0-7603-2647-9
  1. Crocheting. 2. Needleworker's--United States.
I. Cornell, Kari A.
  TT820.H793 2006
  746.43'4--dc22

                2006014630

Editor: Kari Cornell
Designer: LeAnn Kuhlmann

Printed in China

Cover Art
Top photo © Loretta Hostettler/iStockphoto;
Bottom photo © Joy Prescott/iStockphoto.

Permissions
"It Most Certainly *Is* My Grandmother's Crochet…" by
Annie Modesitt was first published as a shorter column in the
fall 2005 issue of *Interweave Knits Crochet*. Used by permission
of the author.

Contents

Chapter One **LEARNING TO CROCHET**

Chapter Two **GRANDMOTHER'S CROCHET**

Chapter Three **AND THROUGH IT ALL, WE CROCHETED...**

Chapter Four **THE ART OF CROCHET**

Chapter Five **CROCHET IN THE SPOTLIGHT**

Introduction

Coming around to the idea of learning to crochet took me a while. I had a tough time learning to knit, and the thought of feeling clumsy again, this time with a hook in my hand, held me back. Plus I felt as if I were just getting into the groove of knitting. I was tackling complicated color work and new stitch patterns. I approached every new project as a challenge to try some new technique and build my skills in the process. Why I didn't think of crochet as a new skill to add to my crafting repertoire, I don't know, but I didn't. I had it in my head that knitters didn't crochet unless they needed to add a decorative edge to a sweater or wanted a fun little flower to tack to a hat.

Then, about six months ago, I spotted the most amazing granny-square blanket displayed in the window of a Stillwater, Minnesota, antique store. I'd seen a million granny-square blankets over the years, but this one was different. The vibrant-colored centers shimmered within their black frames, much like stained glass catching the early morning sun. I studied the stitches and the colors through the window. And that was it. What better motivation did I need to finally learn to crochet than to be able to make a granny-square blanket out of my unused pile of yarn remnants?

So when I was at the Stitches Midwest knitting conference in Chicago a month or so later, you can bet I jumped at the chance to take a quick learn-to-crochet class from Gwen Blakely Kinsler. I took my seat in the front row, and Gwen handed me a ball of soft, baby blue yarn and a size G crochet hook. Around eight of us, all of varying skill levels, showed up for the class. Gwen stood at the front of the group with her back to us, holding her crochet hook and yarn above her head for everyone to see. She made a slip knot and began to hook a single chain, explaining each step as she went along. Then she made the rounds, sitting down and spending time with each student to make sure she was following along.

The hook felt a little awkward in my hands at first, but it wasn't nearly the struggle I remember having when I tried to balance two knitting needles in my hands for the first time. With a simple slip stitch, the yarn was on the hook and I was off and running. The repetitive motion of

GS

Hooked

catching the working yarn with the hook, gently turning the hook towards me, and pulling it through the existing loop was soothing and addicting. Making a single chain was a kick—I was feeling like I could have chained all day long (well, maybe not, but you know what I mean).

Even I realized, though, that my tension was all over the map. Gwen showed me how to wrap the working yarn around my left-hand pointer finger a couple of times and told me to simply "tap" my finger when I needed to release more yarn. At first this felt a little like trying to walk and chew gum at the same time, but then I started to get the hang of it, and loops of uniform size began to emerge from my hook. We moved on to single crochet, half-double crochet, and double crochet before the session was through. I struggled a little with knowing where to plunge the hook to create the next stitch. And sometimes I had a hard time squeezing the hook through the loop. Tension again. I had been a very tight knitter as a beginner, so it would make sense that my crochet would be tough as nails, too.

For the rest of the day I was on top of the world. I had learned a new skill, a skill I had been wanting to try for some time. When I returned home from the show I dug my size G crochet hook out of my knitting bag. I had purchased the hook a couple of years back to pick up dropped stitches

Introduction

in my knitting. At the time I paid no attention to the size of the hook—as when I selected my first knitting needles, I was most drawn to the color: My first knitting needles sported red ends, and, being partial to red, my first crochet hook was a brilliant metallic red. Now I couldn't wait to see what that red-hot hook could do.

Christmas was looming, and I had a couple of knitting projects to finish up before the holiday, but I found myself pausing during the scarf I was knitting for my husband to doodle around with the crochet hook. I crocheted a long chain in a soft, light blue alpaca I had laying around and then dove into a row of single crochet. Hunched over the diagrams in Judith Swartz's *Hip to Crochet*, I tried my hand at the half-double crochet next. I clearly wasn't turning chain, because my little swatch of fabric had begun to curl in on itself, creating more of an oval than a rectangle. It wasn't right, I knew, but unlike a messed up swatch of knitting, which can be downright homely when riddled with dropped stitches, add stitches, and split stitches, this little swatch was somewhat appealing. In fact, it reminded me a little bit of the whimsical blanket pictured on the cover of this book.

I was hooked. I concentrated on catching the working yarn and pulling it through the live loop or loops. That night, I never did return to the straight-laced, basic stock-inette striped scarf I was knitting for my husband. It held no allure for me now. At around midnight, my husband poked his head into the office where I was sitting on the floor, crochet hook flying.

"Are you planning on going to bed anytime soon?" he asked.

"Oh," I mumbled, coming out of my trance just long enough to glance up at the clock. "Yes. I guess I lost track of the time."

The next day, I forced myself to hunker down and finish the knitting projects, allowing myself only a few crochet breaks over the next month. The striped scarf I knit for my husband went perfectly with the hat I had knit him a couple of years before. The light green garter-stitch baby blanket with a dark green sawtooth edge was a hit at my sister-in-law's baby shower. And I finished the light green and blue striped hat for my new nephew Stewart just in time to keep his head warm on Christmas Day. All missions accomplished, all just in the nick of time.

With the holidays and those gifts behind me, I sat down the other night and chained on. I crocheted for a couple of hours with one of the new crochet hooks my mom had given me for Christmas, not making anything special, just getting used to the feel of the yarn slipping through my fingers and the hook in my hand. Next week I will start a three-session beginning crochet class at my local yarn shop. I haven't taken a class in close to a year, and I'm looking forward to hammering down the basics— and to learning how to make that granny square.

I wouldn't be entirely truthful if I didn't admit that reading the essays in this book also inspired me to take up crochet. As I gathered stories for *Hooked: A Crocheter's Stash of Wit and Wisdom*, I was touched by the enthusiasm crocheters have for their craft, amazed by the wide range of crochet stitches out there, and encouraged to hear that crochet is still being passed down from one generation to the next.

So I'm thrilled to present this book, filled with more than twenty stories about crochet, written by professional crocheters, designers, and those who crochet just for fun. The stories range from the sentimental to the whimsical and fun, with a few Zenlike reflections on the craft in between. In "No Bed of Roses," author Amy O'Neill Houck writes of finding an unfinished crocheted blanket, consisting of rose-decorated blocks, stuffed under her grandmother's bed as the family was cleaning out her house after her death. The blanket had obviously been a labor of love, and Amy, who crochets herself, vowed to connect the squares and complete the blanket, despite her busy schedule. Fiber artist Karen Searle reveals how she came to use a combination of crochet and knitting in her one-of-a-kind sculptures that celebrate life and the female form. Nilda Mesa describes the nose warmer she made for her father. Two contributors, Sigrid Arnott and Jennifer Hansen, write about the fun of unearthing vintage crochet doilies, hot pads, aprons, and sweaters at garage sales and thrift shops, and how those found relics inspired them in their own work. And, of course, the book would not be complete without the stories of learning to crochet, sometimes at a grandmother's knee and sometimes not. My hope is that you enjoy them all.

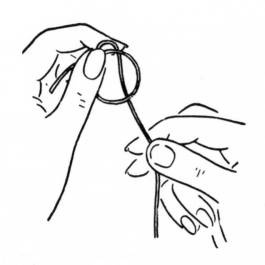

Chapter One

LEARNING TO CROCHET

It was my friend Jan who taught me to crochet.... In a several-hour session at her home, Jan taught me the basics. I went to the craft store, bought some yarn, and within a week I had crocheted a massive, uneven, and very ugly blanket. By the time that blanket was done, I had discovered the rhythm, mindset, and muscle memory of crochet. To my absolute amazement, I had become a crocheter.

—*Jennifer Hansen*, Knitting Yarns and Spinning Tales, 2005

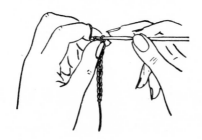

Stories of learning to crochet abound. Whatever the experience, memories of the person teaching the lesson often remain long after the mechanics of crochet have become second nature. Many people learned the traditional way, at their grandmother's knee. Others picked up the craft under the guidance of a family friend. And those who took up crochet later in life may have learned from a college roommate or from an instructor at the local yarn shop. For those who learned at a very young age, the actual lessons have faded with time, but the seemingly innate skill remains. All of the stories collected in this chapter tell the universal tale of learning to crochet, but, as you may expect, each story is unique.

One Loop at a Time

by Deborah Robson

DEBORAH ROBSON DOESN'T REMEMBER learning to crochet. She picked up the basics without being aware of it, and messed around with hooks and books to figure out a number of the traditional ways in which the technique has been interpreted in different times and places. Crochet is, in her opinion, one of the most playful ways to do things with yarn.

She edits and publishes books on traditional textile crafts through Nomad Press and middle-grade novels through Dogtooth Books. The editor of *Spin-Off* magazine for a dozen years, her own writing has appeared in *KnitLit (too): Stories from Sheep to Shawl . . . and More Writing about Knitting*; *KnitLit the Third: We Spin More Yarns*; and *The Knitter's Gift*. She is also a contributing editor for *Pilgrimage*, a nondenominational spiritual literary magazine.

W hat is it about crochet? The skill seems to have been with me almost forever, like knowing how to tie my shoes. I specifically remember learning to knit: where I was, how far my feet dangled from the floor, who taught me. I remember my introduction to weaving, each phase: equipment, fibers, locations. I also remember the details of braiding, bobbin lace, basket-making, macramé, sprang, and other yarn-to-object transformations. But wielding the hook to produce a crocheted chain feels like core knowledge, akin to the sewing needle's dip—and rise to create the running stitch.

My friend Judy, who neither knits nor crochets, tells me that even she once knew how to use a crochet hook and could probably resurrect the awareness. She thinks the most fundamental loop-through-loop understanding floats through kid culture, surfaces at camp and in Scouts and in the classroom.

Because crochet requires a single strand of yarn or string and one simple, inexpensive tool, for which you can substitute fingers at the beginning, there's something about the technique—one loop after another—that makes it seem nearly ubiquitous, and therefore overlooked, in growing up. As far as I can tell, the core movement of crochet may be inhaled with first breath, or acquired with the initial lurching steps, or at the latest learned along with the alphabet.

A few of us keep pulling up loops after the rest of the kids have been distracted by softball or soccer. I don't

17

remember learning the further types of crochet stitch any more than I remember the initial chain, but some of us do move on, piling one loop on another. We slipstitch back into the chain, coaxing a fabric of increasing heft out of the sinuous cord. Perhaps we stay here and master the artful construction known as shepherd's knitting or Bosnian crochet, but many move to the next stage and tease a loop through each base loop and leave it on the hook as we pull through the loop-that-moves-forward, building cloth that expands more quickly and has a bead-like texture. Then we add a spiral of yarn around the base of the hook before we dive into the chain and bring up a loop and go for the stitch-completing pull-through.

Soon we can swivel and plunge through a whole array of closely related options: single, double, treble, quadruple, and the half-step increments between. Exactly what you see when I offer those names depends on where you learned to crochet. A single here is a double over there. That's because the words matter little except when we want to explain to someone else how we maneuver the hook and the strand. The essence of crochet seems to live in a pre-verbal part of the brain.

We construct simple fabrics with our variously sized building-block stitches. Then our visions grow more complex. We alternate, we group, we combine. We invent clustered and angled forms that open doors to intricate textures and three-dimensional shaping.

I have vague memories of using books to figure out shells and granny squares and the encrustations of Irish-crochet flowers and the flat-and-flexible pictorial gridwork known as filet. Hairpin and broomstick and Afghan, or Tunisian, crochet seemed to be other techniques entirely, ones that simply used a hooked tool as an adjunct. They inhabited adjacent territories; they spoke different languages with common roots.

I suspect that many people who continue to keep a crochet hook handy retain a pronounced ability to improvise; we think neither more nor less about what we're doing when we grab the hook and a bit of string than we think about choosing to walk or skip or run. We bring a destination to mind and launch forth on a direct or a meandering path. *Gw*

This makes me wonder why I so often turn reflexively to knitting, why my immediate reaction to "I need a hat" is "cast on," rather than "chain 4 and join in a circle." It seems that crochet is an island offshore and knitting is the continent.

Perhaps this is because knitting is older than crochet, although neither is, as far as we can tell, anywhere near as old as weaving. Spinning, of course, is about as old as textile skills get, although some fiber manipulations don't require twisted strands. People who have researched crochet report finding no evidence of the technique before the nineteenth century. Historically speaking, crochet as a method of giving form appears to be astonishingly young—as far as we know. I wonder where I get the sense that crochet is, or could be, ancient and everywhere.

While thread or yarn is the material most commonly associated with all the fiber crafts, it's not essential. A backward look suggests the important role that materials play. You can weave with reeds or grasses or supple branches. You can crochet, too, with the more pliant of these, splicing and joining to keep the movement alive. Knitting begs for longer strands, for continuity, for spun fiber. Crochet revels in length but doesn't require it.

And who the heck first figured out spinning? Someone sat on a rock fiddling with a tuft of sheep's wool or dog hair or a snag of mountain-goat hair pulled from a bush, or else fingernailed long strips from the stem of a plant. This person idly twirled the stuff between her or his fingers, then realized the game could be extended by adding another clump and continuing to twist. Whiling away the afternoon in the desert or tundra or forest or plains, this adventurer found that the resulting object had acquired strength: You could tug on both ends and the fibers wouldn't drift apart. Someone discovered that ropes fierce enough to lift boulders or haul trees could be evoked from fine fragments.

Similar playful experimentation may have led to the invention or happenstance of crochet: Fingers make a loop, then pull another through it, then another. The hooked tool would have come along later, first to speed the looping chain and then to open the possibilities of working back into already-formed loops. The hook forged the transition from cord to cloth.

How does crochet differ from, diverge from, the other ways in which we work strands of fibrous material using tools that can be whittled into shape by the evening fire?

Crochet likes a long strand: You could, if you chose and had a prolific enough source, chain forever. Unlike most fiber techniques, crochet could utilize an infinite piece of yarn.

Crochet relishes radical changes in direction: Although the work proceeds one loop at a time, each new bight can pounce forward anywhere, can even revisit its source.

Crochet likes a stroll around the block: It will participate in the making of pot holders or mittens.

Hooked

Crochet adapts to the need at hand: It can be used to net fish or hammock a body or lead a horse.

Crochet refuses to be fenced in: There is no limiting number of foundation stitches; it is not constrained by an essential armature, like knitting needles or a loom; there is no pillow; bobbins are not required; there is no need to comb out tangles.

In crochet, the basic component is tiny and yet self-sufficient: Each loop is complete at the same time that it contains the seed's promise of blade, blossom, or tree. And that's why, when you think about it, crochet plays a game whose rules and goal lines change with every movement: a game with no out-of-bounds, a game that perfectly balances control and freedom.

Open a door, open a loop: Walk out to discover the wider world, raise a single, tiny, bent strand.

What will come next?

The only way to find out is to step forward, to pull up the next loop.

Crochet Class

by Holly Laibson

IN THE FOLLOWING ESSAY, crochet instructor Holly Laibson writes about the ups and downs of learning to teach crochet and, perhaps most importantly, the life lessons she has learned from her students/friends along the way. A fanatic crafter, Holly is also a mom and grandma who lives in New Jersey with her husband. She teaches a variety of crafts classes, including mosaics and polymer clay work. She loves them all, but crochet, which she learned from her mom, is closest to her heart.

L ined up on my desk, above my computer, are a series of holiday cards with smiling faces of children and dogs. Each one is from one of my crochet students. I feel so lucky to be part of their circle and to be able to help them express the creativity that is in all of us and often cries to come out.

I *have* to crochet. I do lots of crafts that I really enjoy, but I *have* to crochet. I learned as a child, from my mother, and

Crochet Class

I've been crocheting ever since. Teaching crochet has added a wonderful layer to my life. Several years ago I was asked to fill in for someone and teach a crochet class for my local community school. Thinking it would be fun and something I could do easily, I said yes. That decision changed my life.

I started with a beginner class and kind of winged it. I knew how to crochet really well, so how hard could it be? All right, stop laughing—I admit it, it was really hard. I learned a lot from that first class. How to help someone who has learned one or two stitches but can't read a pattern, how to teach a left-handed student, how to deal with the personality of a class, how to handle a student who has no belief in her abilities, how to quiet a student who whines and complains, how to deal with a student who annoys the rest of the class and the teacher, and how to keep the class interesting and fun. Most importantly, I learned how to handle with my own nervousness at facing a class of women I didn't know, all of whom expected me to be the "The Crochet Expert." Fortunately, they all learned to crochet, and with each class my teaching skills have improved. Now I love to watch someone come into a class with no idea of how to crochet and leave "hooked" on the craft.

The main reason I enjoy teaching is the dynamics of each class. I have discovered that learning crochet is only part of the reason that people come to my class. They also want to be with other creative people, they want to enjoy two hours away from the stresses of family and jobs, and they want to socialize. Each class is filled with fascinating personalities, all with different needs and learning styles. It's my job as a teacher to help the class become a group, find the common bond that will pull them all together. I need to make them want to come each week, not only to learn to crochet, but also to see their new friends and have two hours of comfortable companionship. Sometimes it's a challenge. Some classes gel better than others, but I consider the compatibility of the class and the comfort level of each student as important as learning the art of crochet.

I teach three or four crochet classes a week and enjoy each one, but I have one class that is my greatest pleasure. They started out as beginners in different classes, continued in my intermediate class, and ultimately ended up together. Most of the women in the class are young mothers, not too much older than my own daughter. They needed a night out and a way to express their creativity. Over the several years that they have been coming to my class, they have produced an amazing amount of crochet. Scarves and hats and baby booties, blankets, bibs, and sweaters and more scarves appear on a weekly basis. They share their ideas, and where to get what yarn, and "Oh, I'll pick that up for you" and "Guess what my husband did last night," and they bring their newborn babies to class for everyone to hold and love. They support each other through crochet projects, the challenges of motherhood, husband issues—lots of husband issues—and in life in general.

Janine is a young woman who has had two liver transplants and has a child with a disability. She is a fabulous crafter; she makes jewelry, does stamping, and makes delicious candy. (My personal favorite is her peanut butter cups, and when she brings them to class I eat way too many.) She has become an excellent crocheter. When her son was a ring bearer in a wedding, we searched for a crochet pattern for a ring bearer's pillow. We found a pattern, and her son was a star at the wedding. She is always making things for other people, and her skills are top-notch. She has recently sold some of her crochet work. She works tirelessly for her son's school and has projects going all the time. Janine is the student who anchors the class. She is always there, always ready to help other students with their projects, and if she misses a class someone pulls out the cell phone to call her to make sure she is all right.

Rachel is a young mother of three boys and a girl and a new addition, a Bernese mountain dog. The children are very close in age, and Rachel loves to get out of the house on Wednesday nights. She crochets gifts for all the teachers, bus drivers, coaches, babysitters, and her family and friends. When Rachel had her last baby (a girl, finally, after three boys), she brought her to class, and everyone held her and loved her as if she were a niece. Rachel is always willing to have us in her home and feed us, and, despite her very busy and sometimes overwhelming life, she always comes to class with a smile on her face. She helps others with their crochet projects, lending her skill with technique and yarn and color choices.

Mary Ann has two children and works from her home. In the beginner class she would come each week with a stack of hats and scarves that she had made during the week. No one could figure out where she found the time to do all of that work, and the class was ready to start throwing things at her because she was so prolific while they struggled with one simple project. She continues to produce wonderful items for her children and herself, as well as gifts for teachers, family, and friends. Mary Ann is never afraid to try a difficult project, and she is always successful.

Sarah has nieces that she adores and two dogs, Spike and Angel, both a hugely important part of her family. We all met the dogs when she hosted the class in her home, and we decided that you have to be careful about what you name your dogs. Spike is a little nipper and Angel is an angel. Of course we all became aunts to Spike and Angel too, and when Angel had health problems we all worried as if she were part of our own family. Sarah crochets nonstop for her nieces, making blankets, sweaters, and ponchos. She also makes the occasional dog sweater for the other kids in her life. There is a particular alphabet baby blanket that almost everyone in the class has made at least once, and Sarah sold one of hers. Although she has a very challenging job, she manages to produce a lot of beautiful crochet work.

Hannah just had a baby girl and has an older daughter as well. When the new baby was born, we were honored to be on the e-mail announcement list and thrilled when Hannah brought the baby to class to be cuddled and loved by her honorary aunts. When Hannah was in the beginner class, she was really discouraged after the first class. She felt as if she wasn't going to be able to learn to crochet. I was really pleased that she came back and kept working on it. She has made beautiful baby blankets for all her friends and sweaters for her older daughter. Hannah was back in class a week after having the baby to work on a blanket for the new little one. She looked fabulous and was the envy of all of the rest of us who held on to our baby fat a lot longer than a week.

Josie joined the class as a beginner. She had been told by a quilting teacher that she was "craft challenged," so we have both worked long and hard to rebuild her self confidence as a crafter. Her greatest accomplishment to date is a blanket that she crocheted for her son. He entered college this year, and she wanted to make a blanket in his school colors before he left for his freshman year. Josie not only finished the blanket in time, but she also changed the design to make it more to her liking. The entire class was cheering her on throughout the project. Now no one, including with Josie, would consider her to be "craft challenged."

Two new women have recently joined the class, and we've welcomed them with open arms. Like me, Laura and Theresa are older with grown children, so we get to give a little mothering advice—of course, only when asked. Laura and I discovered that our daughters knew each other in Hebrew school even though we don't remember ever meeting. She is a knitter who picked up crochet very quickly and has already finished some beautiful projects, managing at the same time to plan and carry out her daughter's wedding. We all can't wait to see the pictures.

Crochet Class

Theresa is a very busy woman who gives a lot of time to her grandchildren and to her community. She has a poncho and slippers and a yarmulke on the hook, all projects for her grandchildren.

These are women who would never have met if it weren't for the crochet class. Now we are our own little family. Everyone looks forward to Wednesday nights, and when someone misses we always have to catch up on the family news and yes, the family gossip. We know a lot about each other, and we all really care about each other.

I feel lucky to have had a chance to fill in as teacher of a crochet class several years ago. Without that opportunity, I never would have been a part of this family of crocheters and fabulous, loving women. They have brought joy and inspiration to me in my life and in my crocheting. They have motivated me to grow. I constantly challenge myself to come up with new ideas and designs for the class, and I've even started sending designs out to publishers over the years. I have made more and more difficult projects and delved into new crochet techniques to enrich the class. My life has become fuller, more creative, and multifaceted since I decided to teach. Crochet is in my life, and I can't imagine life without it.

Carrying on the Family Tradition

by Andrea Lyn Van Benschoten

ANDREA LYN VAN BENSCHOTEN came to crochet later in life, but she traces her roots back to her grandmother, who filled every spare moment with crochet. In her essay "Carrying on the Family Tradition," Andrea tells of coworkers who get together over lunch to crochet and end up building lasting friendships in the process.

Andrea has been crocheting for several of years and discovered freeform crochet in the past year or two. She teaches crochet in a number of adult schools and yarn shops and is currently the editor of *Chain Link*, the newsletter of the Crochet Guild of America, of which she is an associate professional member. She lives in Rockaway, New Jersey, with her husband, Glenn, and her cockatiel, Mendelssohn. In 2005, she received a blue ribbon at the New Jersey State Fair for one of her free-form pieces, entitled *Bubblegum and Ladybugs*.

Carrying on the Family Tradition

As a child I watched my grandmother with wonder as she crocheted, creating fabric by running yarn across a hook. On Sundays after dinner, when the men would move to the living room to watch football, the women would sit around the table, reading the Sunday paper, and my grandmother would attempt to show me how to crochet a chain. Of course, as a child I was fidgety, and I quickly lost interest in the task at hand. Many years later when my grandmother passed away, I felt as if I had lost the opportunity to carry on the family tradition. It is one of the great regrets of my life. I have several crocheted items handmade by my grandmother, and I consider them some of my most prized possessions.

Years later, when a few women at the company I was working for planned a craft boutique, I made a few items to sell. We thought this would be an interesting way to show off the creativity of the employees while getting some Christmas shopping done at the same time. I made a few basic crafts to sell—pinecone turkeys, silk-flower wreaths, and potpourri sachets. While sitting at my table, I chatted with Eileen Whitmore, a fairly new employee, about how I had missed the opportunity to learn to crochet from my grandmother and had always wanted to give it a try. She too had been wanting to learn and remembered hearing

Hooked

that Jean Miller, a fellow colleague who crocheted, might be willing to teach us. Well, Jean was game. She told us to purchase a skein of worsted weight yarn and a size G crochet hook. We planned to get together at lunchtime for our first lesson.

Well, I was so excited I sent out what our newfound teacher jokingly called the "all-points bulletin" informing half the division that Jean was willing to teach crochet and anyone interested should meet in a conference room at lunchtime to learn. About ten people showed up for the first lesson. We all joked about how relaxed crocheting was supposed to be while we desperately tried to force the hook through a ridiculously tight chain. Each of us attempted to make a scarf, but we all ended up with triangles after repeatedly dropping stitches at the end of each row! It took me close to three weeks to figure out how to do a successful single crochet, but I was committed to learning, and I always kept my grandmother's memory close by. Not too long after learning my basic stitches, I finished a scarf, complete with fringe. It wasn't fancy by any means, but I knew I had found my artistic calling.

As each week passed, I became more confident in my stitches and more steady in my gauge. I became obsessed, crocheting almost every night after work and most days at lunch. I would regularly pull out some of my grandmother's items for inspiration and to feel her presence as I worked on my projects. I made blankets, tea towels, and scarves, always trying to improve. I very rarely missed a Tuesday session, looking forward to sharing my current project and new successes. Each time one of us learned a new stitch or technique, we would be sure to share our new knowledge with the other members.

After about six months of lunchtime meetings, Sue Boyd, another colleague, told the crocheters she heard a report on talk radio about knit and crochet groups popping up all over the country. The groups were commonly referred to as "stitch and bitch" groups. Well in our case the name stuck! It seemed especially appropriate for our group since we would often bitch about our jobs while we stitched our projects together. We took the nickname to heart and established a hierarchy of members. Jean, our fearless leader, became known as the "head bitch," while I came to be called the "assistant bitch," since I organized our weekly meetings.

Our first year rolled by, and we continued to meet faithfully once a week over lunch in whatever available conference room we could find. We learned the basic stitches such as single crochet, half-double, and double crochet and made scarves, hats, and blankets. We encouraged each other when we had difficulty reading patterns and celebrated each completed project, complimenting the creators on their even stitches and how far they had come since first learning to crochet. As we all progressed in our abilities, a few members decided to give knitting a try. We would regularly discuss knitting versus crochet, comparing the different styles of fabric each produced and how long it would take to finish a garment, but I stuck with crochet. I attempted a knitting project once, but I didn't feel the same connection I felt when creating garments in crochet.

Our crochet group gained quite a bit of notoriety in our division and would be regularly brought up during the company meetings. The president of our location mentioned the group during a meeting about morale and was quoted as saying, "Hopefully, this new initiative will improve morale, so there will be less bitchin' and a lot more stitchin' on Tuesday lunch meetings!" The whole group cracked up.

As the holiday season rolled around, we decided to have a table at the company's annual craft sale. We all made hats, scarves, and doilies to sell—and sell we did! We collected a pretty penny and decided the best way to spend it was to celebrate with a holiday luncheon. The craft sale and holiday luncheon have since become a tradition that we look forward to each year.

About four years later our "head bitch" decided to leave the company to pursue her crochet full time. We promoted Jean to "bitch emeritus," and I took over as the "head bitch." Jean is now teaching at several adult schools and a county college, as well as continuing to freelance for one of the magazines our company owns. Jean's career move inspired me to give teaching a try as well. My crochet had improved quite a bit, and everyone in our group would regularly comment on how fast I could crochet. I also began experimenting with designing my own patterns. I contacted several community colleges in my area. I mailed twenty-eight letters, received seven calls for additional information, and eventually set up four teaching assignments. A huge personal success! I was beginning to live my art!

I also joined the Crochet Guild of America and was accepted as an associate professional member. The associate professional member program is available to members who aspire to make a living from their art. I was assigned a mentor to provide support and encouragement as I advance in the art of crochet. My mentor also answers questions about making contacts, self-marketing, and business goals.

Hooked

Since that very first meeting more than six years ago over lunch, my company's crochet group has continued to meet once a week, every week. People have come and gone, but our core group has always stayed the same. We joke now about who was the worst beginning student and who took the longest to learn. Some have moved on to knitting, cross-stitch, or quilting, but I have stuck with crochet. I now experiment with free form, Tunisian, wire crochet, and other artistic forms all the while knowing my grandmother is right beside me, helping to guide my stitches.

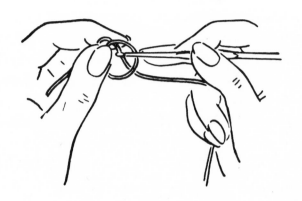

Why Crochet?

by Kay Dorn

IN THE FOLLOWING ESSAY, after many years of asking her mother to complete the crochet portions of her knitting projects, author Kay Dorn signs up for a class and learns to crochet herself.

Kay enjoys knitting for her grandchildren—perhaps there will be some crocheting now that she has learned! In addition to working with yarn, her favorite activities are walking with her husband on Cape Cod, where they live, and volunteering at the Brewster Ladies' Library. Her knitting essays have been published in *Knit Lit: Sweaters and Their Stories . . . and Other Writing about Knitting*; *KnitLit (too): Stories from Sheep to Shawl . . . and More Writing about Knitting*; *For the Love of Knitting: A Celebration of the Knitter's Art*; and *Knitting Yarns and Spinning Tales: A Knitter's Stash of Wit and Wisdom*. She is currently working on a collection of essays called "Things I Wish I Asked My Mother," which she plans to give to her children.

I am a knitter—in fact, I even admit to being an advanced knitter. Everyone I know is aware of it, because they've received a sweater, afghan, or socks with one of my labels that says the projects were made by Grammy, Mom, or Kay.

However, I've not always been truthful about my projects. Ever since I began knitting many years ago, when the directions called for some crocheting—like an edge to an afghan or a button band on a cardigan—I turned to my mother and she did it for me. She did not do this willingly. After each of my requests, she began yet again trying to convince me to learn to crochet myself.

But I couldn't see the need. I preferred to spend my time improving my knitting, not learning a new craft. In the afternoons before my kids came home from school, we'd sit on her backyard double swing facing each other— she crocheting, me knitting.

"It isn't right," she'd say. "If you're going to put your label on a piece then you should complete it yourself."

But I would have completed 99 percent of whatever she finished, and that, I rationalized, was enough to call it my own.

"You'll be sorry for not learning some day," Mom said, "when I'm not here to bail you out."

But when Mom died, my friend Gerry took over crocheting my edges and button bands. At least she didn't nag me about learning to crochet—even so, that didn't totally erase the element of guilt that my mom left hanging over me.

But last fall, due to an unrelated project, I changed my mind about learning to crochet. I had decided to attack that unattainable goal—getting organized. I was tired of piles of magazines sitting in my living room corner waiting to be read, boxes in the basement with clothes I'd never wear again, and an attic so full I couldn't enter it.

I started in the attic.

The first box I tripped over must have been sitting in my attic at least fifteen years. The carton, packed when my dad asked me to sell the house he and my mom had lived in all those years, was labeled "Mom's Crocheting." Emptying their home was such a momentous task that I just piled many of their possessions in labeled boxes and stuck them in my attic. But now the time had come to sort through them.

I opened the box and found *Work Baskets* and other magazines some dating from the 1940s, showing blankets and sweaters that could be made for the soldiers in World War II. I found how-to books and myriad crocheting patterns. Why on earth did she keep them all? But what memories they brought back. All those afternoons on the swing, with my mom trying to convince me to learn crocheting. I

Why Crochet?

could still hear her: "I can teach you to edge in one after-noon." And me answering, stubbornly, "Why?"

I picked up the top magazine in the box—*Magic Crochet*, dated December 1989, Number 63. I started browsing through it and discovered a crocheted table cover that reminded me of one my grandmother made for my *dote* (her Italian for "dowry"). My great-grand-mother, grandmother, and mother were all skilled cro-cheters, probably why my mom wanted me to continue the tradition.

I skimmed the pages, but when I came to page forty-one, I let out a whoop. There was the very pattern that would end a year-long search. The previous year I had bought a lovely evening skirt and shell top, but I needed a long-sleeve, dressy cardigan to wear over it on cool summer evenings. I had searched in all my knitting books, in the library's collection, and my old magazines. I checked online and in Gerry's collection, but could never find just the right one. And there it was! To my surprise, the cardigan was a blend of crocheting *and* knitting. The stockinette sleeves and the entire back, both with twisted ribbing in a different color, were knit, while the two fronts were a delicate cro-cheted lace pattern. It was perfect—except for the fact I couldn't crochet.

Hooked

Well, I could knit the sleeves and back, then ask Gerry to do the two fronts. No, I couldn't even do that, because as I studied the pattern I saw that you started the ribbing by crocheting a chain and knitting into the bumps (whatever they were) of the chain. The pattern called for a contrasting yarn for the chain, which was to be unraveled later. That didn't make much sense to me. Why not just cast on?

Even if I could learn that chain, my conscience would never let me use my label on the sweater if Gerry did the whole front. I'm not *that* deceitful.

Finding that pattern is what finally did me in. I immediately signed up for a crocheting class advertised by a local yarn shop. On the first day of class, Cindy, the instructor, set up her mirror for demonstrating to the one person in our class who was left-handed, then began by telling us how to hold the crochet hook. Well, I couldn't even manage that correctly, but by holding it from the top like my right knitting needle I did fine. Cindy didn't care. The only thing that kept me going through those clumsy first lessons was remembering how awkward the needles felt when my mom taught me to knit those many years ago. Maybe the crochet hook would eventually feel at home, too. That first night we learned to hook a chain, as well as

Why Crochet?

how to single and double crochet. Cindy handed out a list of abbreviations and directions for our homework. Our assignment: Crochet a rectangle measuring ten by fifteen inches, consisting of two rows of single crochet, double crochet for the main body, and two more rows of single crochet at the end.

My first three attempts required undoing. But the fourth time I tried, all went well. I must admit that the rectangle looked more like a parallelogram, but I learned something far more important—ripping out crocheting mistakes was a breeze compared to unraveling rows or picking up dropped stitches to repair a knitting goof. Crocheting might not be so bad after all.

At our next lesson we learned a few borders, and our assignment that night was to edge our rectangle with a reverse single crochet, which Cindy called a crab stitch. It was beautiful, resembling little beads hanging around the edge. Now I'd be able to do my own afghan edging. Hey, Mom, look at me, I thought. No more feelings of guilt!

We went on to make cotton dishcloths, which I promptly crocheted for everyone I knew, then double pot holders. Our "graduation" entailed crocheting small boxes with covers, supposedly for notions. But I made five of the tiny round containers for our grandchildren, filling them with treasures like polished stones for Kristen, wheat pennies for Jake's collection, and a charm for Larisa's bracelet.

Now I was ready to tackle my sweater. I trotted over to the Lady Bug Yarn Shop on Cape Cod, where I live, and picked out a delicious silk-linen-blend yarn in the perfect turquoise color to match the paisley print in my new skirt.

I decided to do my gauge and start with what I knew—the knitted sections. I began with the familiar to get used to working with the yarn. Cindy had shown me how to start knitting from the crocheted chain. She explained this was necessary because later we would pick up the stitches, remove the chain and knit the border in the opposite direction in a different shade of turquoise. This still didn't make sense. Why not just begin knitting in the first place?

"There are many reasons you cast on this way," she said, "I'm surprised you haven't come across this in your knitting before."

Coincidently I did use the technique this past summer when I knit a baby blankie and the beginning border was knit on later. You couldn't tell that it was knit in a different direction, and because I bound off looser than I would have cast on, it allowed all of the borders to be bound-off borders, and they all matched perfectly. Cindy went on to

Why Crochet?

tell me to begin with a chain if you want to add a ribbing, a band, or an I-cord later, perhaps in a contrasting color. She called it an open cast-on, but I have since seen it called a provisional cast-on. So I learned something about knitting from my crocheting instructor, and I was on my way. I knitted the back. Then the two sleeves.

But the project came to the proverbial screeching halt when I studied the *Magic Crochet* directions for the two lace fronts. The instructions may as well have been written in Greek. I needed more help.

Unfortunately, I couldn't find an advanced crocheting course, as it was summer by that time, but I did find one advertised for the next fall—a night-school course for any level crocheter. I signed up, brought my hook, yarn, and an enlarged copy of the crochet pattern, assuming I would learn to crochet the fronts as easily as I made the little boxes. But it didn't happen that quickly. I am still struggling with the sweater, but it is going to be beautiful, and I am so anxious to wear it.

I know that I will crochet more beauties—I've already found a lace scarf pattern I plan to crochet for my daughter's birthday. But I won't give up my knitting. Unlike my previous guilt-ridden thinking, I learned you don't have to do one or the other; the two can complement each other,

Hooked

as proven in this beautiful sweater pattern—a pattern I love, that I happened on accidentally.

But sometimes I wonder if it really were an "accident." My mom wasn't one to keep old things. Unlike me, she was very organized. But I think I know what *really* happened. I can just imagine her perched on her heavenly swing, working her crochet hook and nodding with a smile. She had kept those old books and magazines for a reason. She knew all along eventually she'd find a way to stop me from asking, "Why should I learn to crochet?"

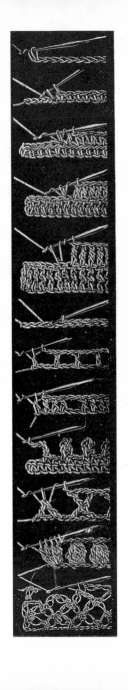

Chapter Two

GRANDMOTHER'S CROCHET

Grandma crocheted slippers for everyone in the family, then made a new pair when the old wore out. Still armed with her crochet hook, she made afghans in blazes of colors—acrylic yellows, lurid reds, tropical lime greens, and oranges better suited for hunting wear. Her afghans featured big patterns that no one could miss: foot-wide stripes and hallucinatory zigzags, multitudes of multihued granny squares, and even one afghan that was simply one huge granny square gone wild. The blankets were Grandma's little nod to luxury.

—*Michael Dregni*, Knitting Yarns and Spinning Tales, *2005*

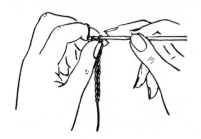

The phrase "your grandmother's crochet" hasn't always had positive connotations. What immediately comes to my mind when I hear the phrase is the television ad for Glade Air Freshener that was popular as I was gathering stories for this book, where the stereotypical grandmotherly woman crochets an air-freshener cozy on the set of a pseudo television program called "Crochet Today." The image doesn't mesh at all with what I've seen of crochet lately—hip, fun designs for shrugs, ponchos, scarves, hats, and even updated versions of the granny square, all emerging from the hooks of crocheters from all age groups. But rather than toss out the old in favor of the new, the stories in this chapter pay warm and cozy homage to the crochet of our grandmothers' generation, with sincere hope that the tradition marches on.

It Most Certainly *Is* My Grandmother's Crochet...

by Annie Modesitt

IN THE FOLLOWING ESSAY, Annie Modesitt laments the use of the phrase "my grandmother's crochet," encouraging today's crocheters to instead embrace the legacy of their grandmothers and pass the tradition on to the next generation. A shorter version of the essay appeared in the Fall 2005 issue of *Interweave Knits Crochet*.

Annie learned to crochet at age six, but didn't publish her first crochet designs until 2000, when a piece combining knit and purl was featured in *Interweave Knits* magazine. Annie's designs have since appeared in *Interweave Knits Crochet* and *Family Circle Easy Knitting and Crochet*, and she is the editor of the 2006 and 2007 Accord Publishing *Crochet Pattern A Day* calendars. Annie's book on knitting and crocheting with wire, *Twist & Loop*, will be published by Potter Craft in Fall 2006.

It Most Certainly *Is* My Grandmother's Crochet

An older family friend taught me to crochet when I was six years old. Crochet lessons were not my choice; my mother felt it would be good for me to take up a pastime that would keep my hands—and maybe my mind—occupied. I was known as a "handy" girl—I was always weaving bits of yarn and string together in bizarre ways and annoying my mother with my oddball creations. My mother hoped to channel this energy into a creative stream that she could easily compartmentalize.

Dropped off at Marie's house on Saturday mornings, I would learn basic stitches, fidgeting as I gazed into the spring sunshine.

After I had conquered the chain and moved on to the single crochet, Marie showed me some basic shell stitches and how to count rows. She didn't have to show me how to sculpt with crochet—that was something that just seemed to come naturally as my stitch count grew and shrank with each row. I was fascinated by the art of cro-chet—the ability to make yarn grow into items that were flat or dimensional, lacy or thickly layered.

Another family friend had attempted to show me knit-ting at around the same time, but that craft didn't come as naturally to my young hands. Perhaps it was the complete-ness of crochet—the fact that each stitch is, in essence, bound off as it is worked, not left live on a needle—that made it easier for me to make crochet my own.

After an hour of crochet Marie would let me run wild outside with some neighborhood kids—exotic because they lived in a different neighborhood in Toledo and we had no friends in common—then I'd come back in for more crochet and a snack.

The Saturday crochet lessons went on for over a year, and by the end of our time together—as much as I loved crocheting with Marie—I enjoyed sitting at the kitchen table listening to Marie's family stories even more. With a cup of tea in front of her, a bottomless glass of milk for me, Marie demonstrated the connection between fiber arts, friendship, and good conversation.

Marie had no children or grandchildren to whom to pass on her passion for crochet; I lived miles from my own grandmother, and my modern mom didn't knit or crochet. I was a student in search of a teacher, Marie was a natural mentor with endless energy for an enthusiastic novice; we filled a space in each other's lives.

For whatever reason, it seems that in our modern times childhood ends very early and adolescence extends through our thirties. The phrase "middle aged" sounds quaint and dated; youth is relative, old age despised.

It Most Certainly *Is* My Grandmother's Crochet

Rank bitterness inhabits our fear of aging, as if no amount of maturing or sagacity could ease the natural process of deterioration. I was fortunate to have Marie, a foster grandmother, to demonstrate the beauty of friendship across generations.

Marie understood that if I didn't grasp a concept the moment she showed me, I would eventually conquer it. Marie was wise—she understood that passion encourages knowledge, but skill develops only with patience.

A phrase entered our vocabulary in the 1980s: "This is NOT your father's Oldsmobile." Adopted by magazine editors, it cropped up throughout the mainstream media to divide a fresh, young generation from the fusty, obsolete establishment. I suppose that eventually it was inevitable that it would be used to separate the new, young, hip movement in the fiber arts from the Red-Heart and plastic- hook old guard.

The phrase "This is not your grandmother's crochet" makes my teeth stand on edge—it's dismissive and simplistic. I understand the sentiment behind the comment— "This is not the dopey, trite, annoyingly kitschy tchotchkes that your grammy produces. This is artsy, fun, and young!"—but the sentiment isn't worthy of the kindness of most crocheters.

Hooked

I'll admit that I've witnessed those whimsically fashioned items that, in retrospect, seem to display at best a rare flare for kitsch and at worst a tremendous lack of taste. Handmade toilet-paper cover antebellum dolls, tangoing frogs, safety orange ponchos worked in Day-Glo, 100-percent-acrylic yarn with size Z hooks. We've all experienced—perhaps endured—similar items.

However, to damn an entire generation of crocheters for a few taste missteps is simplistic and unfair. We wouldn't like future generations to see us as interested in crocheting only string bikinis or tampon holders in five shades of chartreuse.

Marie's home was filled with beautiful handmade items—doilies, rugs, hand-embroidered towels, and aprons. To this day I still use the Christmas stockings she made for my brother and me when we were children.

Along with the lovely items in Marie's home, there were some definite clinkers—crocheted acrylic-yarn pin cushions, pillows worked in astoundingly vile hues, and a multicolored amoeba masquerading as a tea cozy. These were all part of Marie's crochet journey, along with the exquisite and tasteful pieces she created.

It's true that if one is going to stretch the design imagination, there have to be experiments with new

It Most Certainly *Is* My Grandmother's Crochet

fibers, silhouettes, and hook sizes. We look back on an item crocheted in 1974 and wonder, "What were they THINKING!" What they might have been thinking was, "I know this is way out there, and not something I'd usually make, but what a cool stitch!" We need to work outside the box to grow as crafters and not allow ourselves to be stymied by fear of the results—or by the fear that future generations of crocheters may judge us harshly.

We're in danger of creating an atmosphere where established crocheters feel excluded from the new wave of excitement in our craft. Older women have been marginalized for much of our history, but there was always a refuge in the fiber arts, in—as Monty Python put it— "the crochet."

I recently heard of a woman in her early fifties being told at a stitch and bitch gathering that she was "too old" for their group. This is unusual. (My own local fiber group, the Yarrn Pirates, boasts a membership from late teens to senior citizens.) However, this incident emphasizes a divide that is created when we buy into silly phrases like "This is not your grandmother's crochet!" Every generation of crafters will find a way to reinvent the wheel (or the afghan and the half-double crochet) and thus enlarge the craft for all of us.

Hooked

We cannot take ourselves so seriously that we lose our sense of fun or fail to appreciate the glee of past generations. There is wisdom in the handiwork of older crocheters, lessons to learn, techniques to respect—as well as joyful whimsy. Grandma was young once, we'll soon be old.

The crochet I engage in most definitely is my grandmother's crochet—and with any luck, it will be my granddaughter's and grandson's crochet, too!

No Bed of Roses

by Amy O'Neill Houck

IN THE FOLLOWING STORY, Amy O'Neill Houck's memories of learning to crochet at her grandmother's knee all come flooding back when she discovers an unfinished blanket under her grandmother's bed.

Amy has been a yarn fanatic since the age of eight. Her professional career began in 2002 when she formed a fiber-arts cooperative with some good friends, called Neighborhood Knits. Amy has taught knitting and crochet to students from ages six to seventy-six, everywhere from libraries to yarn shops, from classrooms to trains. You can find her patterns and articles online in *CrochetMe*, *MenKnit*, and *SpunMag*. She is a member of the Crochet Guild of America. Amy also maintains a popular crochet and knitting blog called The Hook and I (http://hookandi.blogspot.com) that features stories and patterns, tips, techniques, and book and product reviews.

Entering my grandmother Sitto's apartment after the funeral was a bit like an archeological expedition. The tiny two-room apartment in the Mississippi river town of La Crosse, Wisconsin, was crammed with furniture and knickknacks. It hadn't changed in twenty years. The swivel lounge chair that I loved to spin around in as a child was still there with the same latch-hook flower rug over the back. Sitto still had a turntable, although she hadn't played a record in more than a decade; she never wanted to make the switch to compact discs. Her favorite songs—"Pachabel's Canon," Handel's "Messiah," and Cat Stevens singing "Morning Has Broken"—came on the radio often enough, I guess.

Digging out years of magazines, mittens and hats, grandchildren's and great-grandchildren's school photographs, we sorted and piled—keep, give away, toss. We also all had ulterior motives—to find that one treasure or memento by which to remember her. Aunt Carole sorted costume jewelry and found the rice paper–covered boxes she and Sitto had bought together almost forty years ago in Okinawa. Uncle Jack, the historian, sat quietly searching through papers and found her marriage certificate. My cousin Kate cleaned out drawers of greeting cards and paper napkins and wanted to keep every deck of cards Sitto owned—there must have been fifty of them. Mom searched in vain for letters she had written to her mother when she was in college and jewelry she had

Hooked

given her. Cousin Johanna, the textile artist who's more than a foot taller than Sitto, busily tried on vintage clothes from her closet.

Buried among the dusty boxes of fabric scraps, patterns, and notions, I found a box bursting with Sitto's hand-crocheted afghans, the era of their creation captured forever in the color selection—the earthy brown hues of the 1970s or the bright, primary colors of a blanket made in the 1980s—warm, familiar, and comforting. Because she grew up during the Depression, not a yard of yarn was wasted. Any scraps were turned into what Sitto liked to make best—afghans. Sitto's children and grandchildren all have afghans that she made—zigzagged or shell patterned, with her signature stripe.

My own "Sitto" afghan, with its random stripes of bright color, is hanging over the back of the couch in our playroom. We were unpacking from a move recently when I pulled the blanket out of a box of linens. My five-year-old daughter said, "Mmm—this rainbow-lightning blanket is comfy. Can I sleep with it tonight?" I told her it was at the end of my bed the whole time I was growing up. I took it to college, and it has followed me everywhere. "Sitto made this." She's heard that refrain before. The house is sprinkled with keepsakes made by my Grandmother Helen, my mother's mother, Sitto. In Arabic, "Sittee" means grand-mother, but in our family (we emigrated from Syria in the beginning of the last century) we've always said "Sitto."

When I was little, Sitto would come to our house for long visits in the winter, and we would go spend our summers visiting her and other family members in Wisconsin. Sitto was tiny—under five-feet tall and less than one hundred pounds—but she took center stage when she arrived. When she came to our house, she put on her handmade *mama-san* apron and took over the kitchen. She often brought sweet-smelling snickerdoodle or peanut butter cookies in her suitcase. (I remember one Easter visit when she pulled a frozen leg of lamb out of her suitcase: "It was a bargain, I couldn't pass it up.") She would begin by making *talaymee*—light, airy loaves of soft Syrian bread coated with butter—then *fatyir* (meat pies) or *lubee* (green bean and tomato stew with cinnamon) and *kibbi*, spiced, baked ground lamb with cracked wheat, nuts, and yogurt cheese.

After the cooking was finished, Sitto ironed, she mended, and when it seemed like there was no more work to be done, she sat down. But her hands didn't stop. She reached into her magically bottomless suitcase and pulled out her crochet. Sitto's crochet was never in a fancy yarn

Hooked

bag—she had ancient plastic shopping bags with handles that "clicked" shut, from department stores that no longer exist, with appealing names like Doerflingers and Howlands. The bags were bursting with fat skeins of worsted-weight acrylic or "orlon" in bright red, green, or orange—whichever trendy colors were on sale.

Sitto was a quick crocheter. She made us hats and many pairs of mittens with crocheted chain to hold the pair together. When we were very young the mittens would be threaded through the arms of our coats so they wouldn't get lost. Wearing those mittens on a string made me feel a bit like a marionette. And while the acrylic was warm, it wasn't the best fabric for playing in the snow—ice and wet snow actually stuck to the mittens in larger and larger quantities as we played, so by the time we got home, our mittens were a pair of big snowballs.

Sitto also crocheted dresses and ponchos for me, and bright orange and blue trendy granny-square vests and skirts for my mom in the seventies.

I was fascinated by Sitto's crocheting. All those quick hand movements and loops and pulls mysteriously transformed by her nimble fingers into fabric and garments. Sitto's hands were small but strong—and as long as I knew her, very wrinkled, soft, and olive-toned. Those hands held mine when I was eight years old and finally big enough to learn to crochet. Armed with a small, bright red, hardcover children's crochet book and some yarn, she showed me how to hold the cold aluminum hook (right-handed, even though I was a leftie), how to slide the hook in, catch the yarn, and pull it back out, again and again. As I fumbled over stitches or made knots and tangles she guided, fixed, untangled, and taught. She watched patiently while I created miles of chain, and helped me turn my practice squares into little purses, pillows, and doll blankets.

When she determined I'd mastered the basics—after rows and rows of single and double crochet—she took me shopping to her favorite yarn store, home of the Blue Light Special, K-Mart. I was always attracted to the most hideous variegated colors available. "If you like it, buy two," she'd say, training her little yarn addict to grab another skein of the peachy, seafoam-and-white yarn. Now that I teach formal crochet classes to both children and adults, I'm asked often, "How did you learn?" "My grandmother taught me," I say, "when I was eight years old."

As we were finishing up in Sitto's apartment, I peeked under her bed to make sure there were no other treasures waiting to be unearthed. Tucked away near the head of her bed, there was a small, bulging, white cardboard cake box.

Hooked

The contents, which had been squeezed into place, tumbled out—dozens of pretty and intricate pink, green, and white squares with raised flowers at their center, a hook, a few squares crocheted together, and a skein of white yarn to join them. Creased and yellowed, the pattern had been carefully clipped and glued to a piece of white cardboard (which looked like it had been saved from a package of pantyhose) and hand-labeled "*Family Circle Magazine*, Feb. 1976." It was called "Crochet a Bed-of-Roses Afghan."

Sitto was a collector of clippings, so there was no way of knowing when she actually made the squares—she may have saved the article for twenty years before using it. And the stiff acrylic yarn showed no age, so there was no way to know how old it was. (Sitto hadn't crocheted anything in several years, and her last project was a baby blanket for my daughter who was almost six.) But this was not a scrap project. She must have carefully chosen her colors—they matched the picture exactly. She crocheted each square perfectly, weaving in her ends as she went along. It seemed as if she were working on this afghan simply because she thought it was beautiful, not practical like a hat or mittens. I wanted to know who it was for (a wedding gift or something she always wanted for herself?); I wanted to know why she didn't finish it. Of course, I never will.

No Bed of Roses

There were many keepsakes we saved, and we'll get them home by mail or maybe with a future family road trip to Wisconsin. But I couldn't leave those squares. I carefully packed them all, with the yarn and the hook and instructions, into large Ziplock bags, took them back to my hotel, and did some creative rearranging to fit them all into my suitcase. I wanted to start stitching them together on the plane, but my busy toddler kept me from that. Now that I'm home, I've stacked them in a small basket in the corner of my studio—they're right there, waiting to be worked on, but not out of sight, a frequent reminder of Sitto. In fact, teaching, deadlines, kids, holidays have all kept me from working on those squares so far, but they're always next on my list. And maybe that's what happened when Sitto made them—the pragmatic got in the way of the beautiful and her bed of roses was left unfinished.

Mending a Legacy

by Deborah Robson

IN HER ESSAY, "MENDING A LEGACY," writer Deborah Robson revisits the intricate detail and fine craftsmanship of a bedspread her great-grandmother crocheted as she contemplates how best to mend the damage done by her dog Ariel several years ago.

Deborah edits and publishes books on traditional textile crafts through Nomad Press and middle-grade novels through Dogtooth Books. The editor of *Spin-Off* magazine for a dozen years, her own writing has appeared in *KnitLit (too): Stories from Sheep to Shawl . . . and More Writing about Knitting*; *KnitLit the Third: We Spin More Yarns*; and *The Knitter's Gift*. She is also a contributing editor for *Pilgrimage*, a nondenominational spiritual literary magazine.

My great-grandmother had a love of, and a gift for, color. One of a pair of matching bedspreads that she made has been passed along to me. She crocheted its patterned top in five saturated hues of all-wool knitting worsted: navy, burgundy, a delicate lavender that is the only color in the piece with a slightly grayed tone, a clear red reminiscent of holidays, and, at the heart of each component square, a brilliant color from the extended red family—a shade sometimes found in geranium blossoms.

To call the elements that she assembled "granny squares" tells a crocheter something about their construction, but the afghan that forms the core of the bedspread embodies none of the associated clichés. The images brought to mind by the words *granny square* involve scrap yarn, any convenient hook, and loose construction. None of those characteristics fits this work. In addition, the completed crochet work was lined with a fine red fabric that falls on the spectrum between the clear red and the geranium color. A finer blanket-binding than I ever knew existed was hand-stitched around the perimeter. It's a silk-like rayon, unlike today's polyester version.

I have the impression that the great-grandmother who made this piece was my paternal grandfather's mother. She may have been born in the 1870s. I imagine that she was in late middle age, as I am, when she constructed the two twin-bed–sized spreads. The pieces were not assembled from leftovers. The closely related shades in the work tell me that smooth, consistent yarn in a wide range of

Hooked

colors was available to either accommodate or spur her creative vision.

Sitting on my bed, I hold the comforter still sheathed in the heavyweight plastic zippered case that has protected it for as long as it has been in my house. I don't think of myself as owning it; I don't think we can "own" the work of someone else's hands, whether we have inherited that work or been given it or have exchanged money for the privilege of living with it.

In my family, textiles are to be honored by use. There is no bed in my house where this piece has been able to safely play the role for which it was intended: covering, welcoming, enhancing. So it has rested in a long temporary storage, waiting for a stable phase in my life that would bring it back onto an orderly bed, released from the sturdy enclosure that originally packaged a plain-wool, store-bought, solid-colored blanket that keeps me warm in winter.

I contemplate the damage that has marred my great-grandmother's work despite my care, thinking of how to make as right as possible what cannot be undone. As someone who has spent decades studying and making textiles, I'm acutely aware of what it would take to replicate its several parts.

Mending a Legacy

On the floor next to me lies Ariel, our eleven-year-old border collie, her muzzle white on both sides now instead of just one, a symmetry granted by age. Medication tempers her arthritis and a recent blood test indicates she may need an ultrasound to see how her liver's doing. She won't be with us forever, but she is here now, lying on her side with her legs relaxed toward the bedroom door, a loyal friend in fur.

For the past few months, Ariel has begun to slide up onto the foot of my bed at night after I've turned out the light. I barely feel the futon move, although I sense that she's by my feet, snuggling into the dense wool blanket. She stays for fifteen or twenty minutes, then gently transitions back to the floor, so quietly that I'm often not sure when she's gone. She spends part of the night where she's lying now.

She breathes out, almost a sigh, as I look at my great-grandmother's handwork.

A number of triangular rips in one corner of the plastic case expose the afghan, and I can see that two of the crocheted squares directly beneath those rips have been torn, along with a four-inch section of the soft binding. Easing my fingers through one of the holes in the plastic and beneath the edge of the bedspread, I discover two straight, one-inch tears in the finely woven cotton backing. This cloth, although commercially made, has such a high thread-count that I can't think where I could find its equal today. Contemporary fabric stores abound with colors and patterns that might have seemed garish to my great-grandmother, printed on cloth far coarser and stiffer than this. Her own imagination provided the patterning in her life. The materials are soothing simply to touch. I stroke the backing, thinking that perhaps a mill in Italy still makes cotton this nice. For the equivalent linen, I'd need to go to Belgium or perhaps Ireland. Yard goods of this quality were once readily available, although I have a hard time thinking of them as commonplace.

My great-grandmother brought both proficient craftsmanship and an artist's eye to her work. Her squares resemble the most basic granny square in the way that mortise-and-tenon hardwood construction resembles nailed-together number-two pine. She worked her rendition of the concept at a much finer gauge than most, and her version incorporates more rounds. All of the six-and-a-half-inch squares are identical, and the assembled piece has an overall dark tone, enlivened by those geranium-colored centers. The surrounding darkness makes the centers look like stained glass illuminated from behind.

Mending a Legacy

The visible stitches are double crochets in clusters of three, built from a center ring and growing geometrically in rounds to the outer edges: two rounds of the geranium color, composed of four clusters in the first round and eight in the second; two rows of the holiday red, more common but still not ordinary, twelve clusters and then sixteen; two rows of the grayed lavender that is slightly lighter than the red, an exception to the overall progression toward deeper tones, twenty and twenty-four; then one row each of the burgundy and the navy, twenty-eight and thirty-two.

Because of the way my great-grandmother joined the squares, the navy forms a two-row–wide grid that provides the afghan with a solid integrity, of the sort that I imagine she herself had, if she is the one of my eight great-grand-mothers I think she is. The only portrait I have of her is the soft yet disciplined bedspread in my hands.

On the two torn squares, several clusters of navy, burgundy, and lavender stitches have been ripped from their moorings. In a similar knitted textile, I would know how to heal injuries of this severity. Crochet is, at the stitch level, simpler to construct than knitting, yet the resulting interlacements are more complex to mend. I imagine how I might simulate the double crochets with yarn threaded into a blunt-tipped, large-eyed needle, a tool that would

Hooked

give me access to the stitches in the rows both above and below the ripped sections. Although such a repair would be possible, it would not be graceful.

I call out to my grown daughter, who is working with free weights in the living room, twenty feet away: "Do you remember if it was Ariel who did this?"

She waits the beat of several repetitions and replies, "Yes."

This happened many years ago, and I haven't been able to face a close look at the fractured fabric until now. I think I have developed a technique of forgetting exactly who in the household was responsible for what, a trick of age that perhaps lets us keep loving the beings in our lives.

As a grown dog, Ariel has not been a chewer, except of Nylabones and other sanctioned objects. Mischievous, yes. Destructive, no. When she was a foundling puppy, she tested her teeth on objects I cared about: the afghan; a much-used book that reveals its white interior while still closed because portions of its black cover are missing; my mother's cherry rocker, which she gave me twenty-five years ago so I could sit comfortably while nursing my baby.

"And I didn't kill her?"

"Apparently not." My daughter, now taller than I am, laughs.

Mending a Legacy

I look down at the sleeping black-and-white dog, blue-ribbon holder of an obedience title that required us to work together for several hours a week over many years. She's a good companion, with too much brain and spirit to be perfect.

Textiles don't last forever, I remind myself, even though some outlast humans. Mountains don't last forever, either. They only seem permanent when gauged against other lifespans.

I gently tug the afghan out of the torn case and unfold it to assess the damage in light of the whole. The full spread is 9 squares wide and 13 squares long, a total of 117 squares, and measures about 60 by 85 inches, including the binding.

Viewing the work in its entirety, I ponder my next step. I think I need to find five colors of smooth, all-wool yarn similar to what my great-grandmother used. Then I will figure out how she made her squares, matching my gauge to hers. When I've got the materials and the structure, I will crochet two matching squares, which I will secure over the two broken ones, not replacing but encasing them, keeping them as intact as possible while shielding them with the new work. Because I need to find the right materials to work with, close to the originals in fiber content, color, and texture, it may take a year or more to finish the reparations.

I think there is one company that makes a nice wool knitting worsted in enough colors that I will be able to find something close to what I need. It's not stocked locally. I'll have to drive a hundred and twenty miles round trip to do the color matching. I won't be able to make that excursion this month. However, I have a few partial skeins of the yarn I have in mind, in other colors, and I can work up samples that will let me know if I'm on the right track and that will also let me begin to resolve the technical questions involved in replicating my great-grandmother's work.

It will be harder to find materials to mend the binding and the backing. For the blanket binding, I doubt that I will be able to locate anything comparable, although I should be able to make a serviceable casing out of fabric-store notions for the four-inch damaged stretch. A three-inch square of a moderate cotton should be enough to support the torn pieces of the lining. If the fabric is soft enough and a close-enough color, I can get away with a lower thread count than the original.

I refold the afghan and slide it back into its inadequate shelter, and then do some research to establish a baseline for my test squares. My great-grandmother's variation follows the traditional pattern, but is far more complex than the samples in books or online. Her squares have been much more carefully constructed than those in the photos I find. I learn that some crocheters get their squares to lie flat by working chain-two corners, and some, with tighter working styles, produce equivalent results with chain-three. I'll probably chain two. Maybe later I'll nudge around in my great-grandmother's work and see what she did. For now, all I need to do is find my own equation.

The first crochet hook that I try is a smooth, white plastic one that always feels warm in my hand. It came to me through the family. Its nonhook end has been molded to look like simple wood-turning, with a couple of shallow grooves setting off a small ball shape. These areas were once red, although the shaft and hook have been white all along; ruby shadows remain in the deepest parts of the grooves and along a few smooth surfaces of the rounded end. The rest of the color has been worn away.

When I've worked just two rounds, it's apparent that I'll have to use a marginally larger hook to match my great-grandmother's results. I change to an aluminum hook and begin again.

After a total of three starts, worked and ripped out—chain eight, chain six, and chain four before joining—it's clear that she did not start her squares in a standard way. Her centers are more snugly drawn together than those I'm coming up with.

I decide that my great-grandmother must not have chained her starting rings. Perhaps she wrapped the initial yarn around her index finger several times and then began to double-crochet into that simple curved form, later tugging steadily on the loose end to tighten the circle.

One of my hands guides the dipping and pivoting hook that picks up the yarn and twists it around itself. The other steadies a growing square. I am grateful for my love of color; for the pleasure of intricate, closely worked, and supple fabrics; and for the stitches, looped up and rotated one at a time, that hold together generations with a strength that belies the easily sundered materials that we use.

I'm glad to have this textile within touching distance and content that over the decades I've acquired enough knowledge to mend it. I sit crocheting at the crossroads where fate, in the afghan's encounter with puppy teeth, meets what might be considered destiny—an inclination, carried by a dominant gene, to work with yarn and fabric.

Ariel rolls over on her back, exposing the soft white fur that covers her pink belly, which rises and falls with each deep, sleeping breath.

A Family of Designers

by Marty Miller

IN THE STORY THAT FOLLOWS, Marty Miller traces the path crochet has traveled in her family, from her Ukrainian grandmother, to her mother, to her sister, and finally to her own granddaughter.

Marty is a crochet and knitting designer, and her patterns are published in various books and magazines, including the Crochet Guild of America's *Pattern Line*, *Interweave Crochet Magazine*, *Family Circle Easy Knitting and Crochet Magazine*, *The New Crochet*, *Fabulous Crocheted Ponchos*, *Michaels' Book of Needlecrafts*, and *100 Hats to Knit and Crochet*. She considers a day without crochet a day without sunshine. Marty is also a group exercise instructor and personal trainer.

I've pieced together my grandmother Tillie's story from old memories, both mine and those of my siblings and cousins. Tillie came to the United States from Ukraine in 1898, when she was thirteen years old. This was a time when Eastern European countries were

A Family of Designers

becoming inhospitable and dangerous for Jews. Many older daughters of Eastern Europeans came to the United States during this time to earn money so that they could pay for the rest of the family to come and settle in this new country. Because of some mix-up in passports, family lore has it that Tillie had to be disguised as a boy until she arrived. This meant cutting her long hair and dressing in boy's clothes—pretty traumatic for a thirteen-year-old. She left most of her family in Ukraine, and traveled with another family or her sister's family to America. Once here, she moved in with an aunt who had been living in New York City for a while. Tillie got a job in a sweatshop operating a sewing machine, and didn't have time to learn to read or write English, a common occurrence during this wave of Jewish immigration. My grandmother eventually married and started her own family. She had two sons and a daughter, my mother.

Years later, when my grandfather died, my grandmother came to live with my family. While my parents worked, Tillie took care of my brother, my sister, and me. She continued doing what she had done for others all her life—sewing clothes for us and crocheting doilies and tablecloths for the household. My sister remembers Tillie making us matching outfits when my brother celebrated his bar mitzvah. She looked in the window of a fancy children's store, found an outfit she liked, and designed our clothes to match. She didn't need directions—she couldn't read them anyway. This was also the way she crocheted and knitted. She saw something she liked and copied it, or designed her own similar piece. I have some of her doilies, pot holders, and tablecloths, and I often look at them with awe. Tillie was the first designer in our family, and her designs are timeless and beautiful.

When my mother was a little girl, Tillie taught her to crochet, and when I was a little girl, probably five or six, Tillie taught me to crochet. (My sister is left-handed, and my mother tried to teach her, but couldn't. I finally taught her a couple of years ago.) I remember crocheting a doll blanket out of light blue (my favorite color) worsted-weight yarn when I was seven or eight. When I was in seventh (my sister claims it was actually eighth) grade, I was able to show off my crocheting skills at school when my teacher taught the class how to make granny squares (yes, the entire class, boys as well as girls). We would work on the squares after we finished our class work. When the class had made plenty of squares, we stitched them together to make an afghan for the Korean War veterans. I was one of the few people in class who already knew how

A Family of Designers

to crochet, and I learned the granny-square pattern quickly. I was a fast crocheter and was able to finish many squares—significantly more than a certain boy in my class who always bugged me. (He usually got the same grade as I did, or a little better, and would constantly tease me about it.) This time I got to tease him—sweet revenge.

I remember going home from school and telling my mother that I had learned how to crochet a granny square. My mother knew how to crochet, of course; Tillie had taught her when she was a young girl. But my grandmother worked in thread, so she taught my mother to crochet in thread. When she was younger, my mother made short filet-mesh neck scarves, and I have one of them now that I cherish. My mother had to teach herself to read directions, but she had never taught herself how to make granny squares. So as soon as I told my mom I could make them, she excitedly grabbed her yarn and hook and asked me to teach her. She sat on the couch, and I kneeled beside her. It felt a little strange, showing my mother how to crochet, but she caught on quickly and soon became the granny-square queen of our family. Every child, grandchild, great-grandchild, aunt, uncle, cousin, friend of the family—just about everyone she knew—received at least one granny-square afghan from my mom. And family members received many more than just one. Every new baby had an afghan. For every wedding there was an afghan. And these were not small afghans—they were full size, 140 squares with four different color rounds in each granny square. My mother worked full time, so she crocheted in the evenings. She was quick. It usually took around two weeks for her to complete a blanket. In between, she made sweaters (lots of granny-square sweaters), hats, scarves, buntings, both knitted and crocheted. But her crocheted granny-square afghans were her trademark.

Just out of curiosity, I recently compared one of the granny-square afghans my mother made for me more than thirty years ago to a granny-square afghan I made for myself around the same time. (This was one of my first original designs.) Sure enough, the way my mother made her granny squares long ago was exactly how I made mine and still make them today.

My mother, however, didn't stop at ordinary granny squares. She made squares with popcorn stitches, clusters, and everything else she could think of. She figured out different ways to join the squares—chaining between the squares, crocheting the squares together, and sewing them together. She designed her own edging for the afghans (and her way is still my favorite edging pattern for

A Family of Designers

afghans). Her style was impeccable, and her afghans are still being used and loved.

As I grew up, I was surrounded by crocheting and knitting. One of my favorite pictures of my grandmother and my mother shows them sitting in the living room in big easy chairs, both knitting. My mother is knitting American style, with the yarn in her right hand. My grandmother is knitting Continental style, with the yarn in her left hand. I have always knit like my mother, holding the yarn in my right hand, but just recently, when I had to finish a knit project quickly, I taught myself to knit Continental style. I remember after dinner, my family would sit in the living room watching television. My grandmother and my mother would knit or crochet, while I sat on the floor at the coffee table finishing my homework.

But even though crochet and knitting were part of everyday life, I don't remember crocheting or knitting much myself. Yes, there were the granny squares, and later when I was in college, I knit my boyfriend a scarf (in my school colors, not his) and crocheted him a "nose warmer," which was all the rage back then.

It wasn't until I married the boyfriend from college and became pregnant that I really started to crochet a lot. My

Hooked

mother was going to make my baby one of her granny-square afghans, and I decided to make the baby a ripple afghan. I can't remember if I followed a pattern or made one up (this was a long time ago). I probably got a basic ripple-afghan pattern and changed it to suit the yarn and the size of afghan I wanted to make. I must have taught myself to read patterns by this time, and this first effort was more or less successful. The foundation chain and first rows had a very tight tension, so the afghan's sides flared out a bit, but I was pleased with it, and my baby didn't know it wasn't perfect. (I use this afghan today, to show my students about tension changes and beginning chain problems.) When my son was a little older, I made him another ripple afghan, and I am happy to say I corrected the tension problem. When my son was still a baby, I would crochet when he was napping, and I discovered that I really loved it.

Then a friend of mine, who also had a young son, showed me a pattern for a puppet that she found in a magazine. This puppet had a large mouth that opened and closed, big "bug" eyes, and was sized just right to fit a toddler's hand. We called it the the "monster" puppet. She and I started crocheting puppets and giving them as gifts to our children's friends. The puppets were such a big hit that we decided to make a bunch of different puppets and sell them at a local craft fair. I designed a few different puppets to start, and when the puppets sold, I designed more. They were all "child proof"—everything was crocheted or sewn on, and there were no buttons or other parts that could be hazardous to young children. We also used yarn that was completely machine washable. We made enough money to buy more yarn for puppets and for our own projects, so we felt successful. We kept this business going, selling at craft fairs and co-op craft stores, for about four or five years, until we both moved away and got busy with other things. This was almost thirty years ago, but people still stop me sometimes to tell me that they recognize me from the craft fairs—that they bought a puppet from me, that it is still in good condition, and that they are saving it for their grandchildren.

Over the next few years, I went back to school and had less time to crochet, but I still managed to make bags, hats, scarves, sweaters, skirts, afghans, slippers, capes and ponchos, belts, baby presents, curtains, and anything else I could think of. During this time I also picked up a few tricks—how to crochet a circle, how to substitute yarns without messing up the original design, and how to make a sturdy handle for a bag.

Hooked

I stopped crocheting entirely when I went back to school for a masters degree and then a Ph.D. I just couldn't seem to find any time to pick up a hook. Then when I was in my last year of school, writing my dissertation, my niece adopted a baby. This was the first baby in our family since my mother died, and I wanted to continue the tradition of crocheting an afghan for each new baby. My niece's mother crocheted, but she had also passed away. My sister didn't crochet. I was the only one who crocheted in our family, so it was up to me to carry on the tradition. I told my niece I would make the afghan, but I couldn't start it until I finished writing my dissertation.

The same day that I handed my paper to my advisor, even before I defended it, I went to the local yarn store to look at yarns for the afghan. I was astonished, over-whelmed, amazed, flabbergasted, at all the new yarns. I could not believe the choices. I picked out some acrylic worsted-weight yarns and a new hook. I hoped I could remember how to make a granny square, because, of course, the afghan would have to be a granny-square design. But I planned to make one of my own granny-square designs, not one of my mother's. To my amazement, I went home, picked up the hook, pulled end of the yarn from the center of the skein, and began to crochet as if I

A Family of Designers

had never stopped. I finished that afghan, and I haven't stopped crocheting since.

After I got my Ph.D., I looked around for a place that offered crochet lessons. I wanted to meet other crocheters and thought that this would be a great way to do that, while learning some new techniques. Not finding a crochet class in my town, I began knitting lessons to refresh my knitting skills. Then it dawned on me: "Well, if no one is teaching crochet in town, I should."

I got to know the owner of the yarn store where I took knitting classes, showed her some of my crocheted designs, and asked her if she wanted me to teach. She agreed, and I started. I soon discovered, though, that there were few crochet patterns available using the yarns that the store carried. I began designing my own patterns for my students. Buying the yarn to create the designs, however, cost me more money than I was making, so I contacted a few yarn companies to see if they were interested in buying the designs I had created using their yarns. Only one company responded, asking me to make a bag for them that they needed right away. I agreed, and I was added to their designer list for future projects.

At around this same time I discovered the Crochet Guild of America, where I met other crochet designers and

Hooked

professionals, learned of more opportunities for crochet design, and had more designs published. I became a professional member of the guild, and began to mentor other crocheters. I eventually became chairperson on the guild's professional development committee. That's what I do today: design, teach, and lead that committee. I love what I do.

Whenever I stop to think about it, about how much fun I'm having designing and crocheting and about how lucky I am to be able to do what I love, I think of my mother and grandmother and how their crochet legacy lives on in me. I feel as if they are looking out for me, and I think they are pleased that I am following in their footsteps. What's even more thrilling, though, is watching my granddaughter crochet. She even takes her crochet projects with her when she goes out, just like her grandmother. Crocheting has been passed down in my family, from generation to generation, all the while evolving with the times. My grandmother worked in thread because that's all there was; my granddaughter uses everything because she can "shop" in her grandmother's stash. My grandmother couldn't follow a pattern, and my granddaughter doesn't *want* to follow a pattern. Through all these generations, crochet has been an important part of our family—a family of designers.

Life in the Tundra

by Nilda Mesa

ARTIST, WRITER, DESIGNER, AND RECOVERING LAWYER, Nilda Mesa comes from a long line of crocheters, knitters, spinners, and weavers of Spain. Her work has appeared in *Interweave Crochet*, *Knit Lit Too: Stories from Sheep to Shawl . . . and More Writing about Knitting*, *Knit Lit the Third: We Spin More Yarns*, *Stitch 'n Bitch Nation*, *Knitty*, *Wild Fibers*, and the forthcoming *Stitch n Bitch Crochet*, as well as her popular blog "Waltzing Knitilda." She is at work on a bilingual kids' learn-to-knit book. Her art has been exhibited in New York and France, where she is co-director of a summer artist residency program in Brittany. The rest of the year she lives in Harlem with her husband, two kids, and two cats.

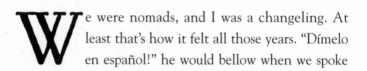

We were nomads, and I was a changeling. At least that's how it felt all those years. "Dímelo en español!" he would bellow when we spoke in English, because we just wanted to be American. No other kids in the tundra on the southwest coast of Lake Michigan spoke Spanish. Maybe their parents and grandparents spoke German, or Polish, or Italian, or even Yiddish. But not Spanish. And none of our friends did.

"Dímelo en español!" would be the answer to our questions, the response to our tales of the school day.

Not every day. Just some days.

Those days when he thought about soft breezes caressing the palm trees. When he talked about Sunday feasts with the aunts and uncles and cousins, a roast pig cooking on a spit for really special days. When he talked about his duties as an altar boy, sweeping out the colonial church. When he talked about his student days at the boarding house and the jokes his friends all played on each other. When he described the glamour of the Copacabana's long-legged showgirls and their feathered headdresses.

Not every day, no. But when the wind chill would hover at minus twenty for a month solid. When yet another blizzard would make the sky, the air, and the ground the same shade of white, for the fifth time in a month. When John Coleman on the Channel 7 news would laughingly compare the high in Anchorage with the high in Chicago for the day, and Anchorage would be warmer. When he would utter those dreaded three words: "Canadian cold front."

Not every day. Those days when he would sing along with Guillermo Portabales, the great folk singer, and realize that we didn't understand the words to his heartbreaking songs. "Cuando llegaré al bohío," came the plaintive verse, with only a bongo and acoustic guitar to keep the soulful voice company. It was a whole song about a worker who left his thatched hut in the middle of nowhere before dawn to work in the sugar-cane fields, and trudging back on his way home after dark realizes he has only one small coin in his palm to show for a day of backbreaking labor. And he wonders when he will get back to his little home, before arising the next day to start the trek once more. All the songs were like that. He knew the words to them all.

It was different with my mother. She was studying at the university to be a teacher and wanted us to grow up without an accent because she knew that Americans always discriminated against foreigners with accents. She was right, of course. He knew it, too. But he thought we could speak both. That we *should* speak both. Given where we were born.

It was different with my grandmother. Not his mother, because she died outside of Havana without my ever knowing her. No, my mother's mother, who remembered words like "Good night, everybody" and "How are you?" and not much else from her happy youth in Greenwich Village. But she wished she remembered and hoped she would pick it up again as we spoke English around her.

She tried hard to remember more English words the summer that I was eight and she taught me how to crochet and knit. With knitting I struggled. Aluminum needles clanging to the floor, split stitches, dropped stitches—I thought I'd never get it. Spanish, English—language didn't make a difference. It was my fingers that couldn't get it.

But crochet? Oh. Well. Now. That was easy. Only one needle *could* drop, and then it really didn't because of that little hook on the end. It was hard even for me to split stitches with that rounded blunt tip, so the hook glided in and out of the loops quickly and smoothly. Row after row, I quickly made blankets for toys. She showed me how to work lengths of chain stitches, maybe eight, maybe ten, however many I thought looked right, and then join them to the row below and do it again. My Misty doll soon had glamorous, long fishnet vests, just like Maude on TV.

As the weather began to turn chilly once more, I began to think of what I would get him for his birthday. My allowance was limited to a miserly ten cents a week, and I was not yet babysitting. Somehow I scraped enough change together for, or, more likely, convinced my mother to add to the cart, some medium blue light-worsted or fingering-weight acrylic from Turnstyle's. Maybe it was Korvette's.

He complained a lot about his nose getting cold when he came in from shoveling. This made an impression on me. I was not yet confident enough to think I could tackle a scarf or one of those balaclava helmet hats. Even in those pre-Freddie days I thought they were scary-looking. But I could make a nosewarmer.

My nose and his nose unfortunately have much in common. They are both rather prominent in just about every one of their three dimensions. So I thought I had a pretty good idea of what needed to be made.

Single crochet, started at the tip of the nose, worked circularly. All the way to the base of the nose. It was probably, oh, about five inches long. Looked about right. Ought to keep his nose from running and turning purpley red.

But the nose warmer wouldn't stay on all by itself. It kept falling off my nose when I tried it on. It needed a strap. Or maybe a tie.

Life in the Tundra

Chain stitch. Such a very useful stitch. Come to think of it, his head looked big too. So I made two lengths of chain stitch, one for each side of the nose, to be tied at the back of his head. His hat could cover up the bits from his ears on back, I thought. Each side was about three feet long. Long enough.

To tassel or not? I think I decided not. I'm not entirely positive, but I am relatively certain that even at that age it occurred to me that his nose needed no additional embellishment.

He was delighted to receive it. Big smiles all around. Too big, as I think back on it. "When are you going to wear it?" I would ask. "Oh, it's not really cold enough yet," he'd say. Or, "I forgot it again." Or, "I did wear it, it's just in my pocket now."

Before I knew it, Father's Day was rolling around. Again, I needed something. Flush with the positive response to the nosewarmer and with quite a lot of the medium blue acrylic in my stash (nosewarmers really don't use up much), I began to analyze what would be another useful gift that could be made out of yarn.

A tie. Of course. He was always wearing them to go to work. He always needed a new one.

Single crochet. About eight feet long should be plenty

to wrap around a neck and cover a button placket without any gaps, with extra for the knot. Decreases that looked like stairsteps on the edges to give it that taper.

But something was missing. Because the tie was for Father's Day, it needed something extra. What more appropriate embellishment than to crochet the letters "D-A-D" on it? Vertically. In white. With an embroidered outline, as they weren't quite crisp enough.

By that time, I was a really fast crocheter and didn't even need to look at my stitches while working. Still, it took forever. And I couldn't really work on it in secret, because then I'd miss too many favorite TV shows. So, when asked, I was vague, cagey even, about its ultimate purpose.

On Father's Day, I had another hit. Once again, smiles all around. Once again, a little too much tooth showing as I think back on it.

I think he wore it to work the following Monday. I'm not really sure. I know he took it to the office with him and proclaimed that all his colleagues were struck dumb with admiration. He liked that. I am not sure how many more workdays the tie saw.

Years went by. Some of them marked with phones hung up, arguments, and ultimately, geographical distance.

Life in the Tundra

Marked as well by weekly phone calls, initiated frequently by my mother. He spoke Spanish to us all, she spoke Spanish to him and English to me, and I spoke English. When they moved to Louisiana, California, and finally Florida, there was no need for a nosewarmer. When they retired, there was no need for a tie. I forgot all about the gifts, except for random family holidays when someone would start the "do you remember when" game.

Then my mother took ill. More and more of her bright, inquisitive, and kind mind seemed to disappear, and it was time for them to move again. He and I took on the task of packing and sorting, mostly out of her sight, as she didn't want anyone going through the things in her house. People wanted to steal her things, she whispered. Maybe even me.

The boxes were endless. My parents didn't throw anything out, because, well you just never know when something would be needed. Even empty boxes, teachers' lesson plans, and electrical circuitry books.

And a medium blue acrylic nose warmer and eight-foot-long tie that said "Dad." They had made it to Florida.

He didn't try them on again. But we both grinned.

To my surprise I can not remember what language we used when we found them. I don't know when the grass began to grow on that frozen battlefield, but it did. In

Hooked

Miami, where he can find lechón down the street, where the soft breezes again caress the palms, and where the sounds of brass sections and bongos are everywhere, he still has the tie and nose warmer.

She's now lost her Spanish as well as her English, but it's the Spanish she understands. As it turns out, these days I speak in Spanish to her all the time, and in Spanish to him much of the time. Though he doesn't have to, he speaks in English to me quite a lot.

And I knit. It's good to be bilingual.

GOLD TIP

Chapter Three

AND THROUGH IT ALL, WE CROCHETED

The crochet makes perfect sense in this climate of alienation and resentment. I can take it with me anywhere, and anywhere I need some form of escape, crochet provides it. This is why the outcome of my work is irrelevant; I am not crocheting to make a tangible thing, I am crocheting to transport myself…. Hook in, loop, and out; with this focus, I can steel my mind against my unease and paranoia.

–Lela Nargi, "*Aquarium Saturdays*," 2006

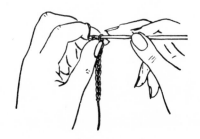

In times of trouble or stress, having something to do with one's hands can make a world of difference. Just having a task on which to focus can pass the time and allow thoughts to either disappear or flow freely. The rhythm of crochet—the repetitive motion of pushing the hook through the next stitch, wrapping the yarn around the hook, and pulling the yarn through the existing loop—can be relaxing. The stories in this chapter reflect on the Zenlike, meditative characteristics of crochet.

Aquarium Saturdays

by Lela Nargi

A RAINY DAY AND THOUGHTS OF CROCHET carry writer Lela
Nargi back to a moment she thought she had forgotten—a
time when the act of crocheting made the unpleasantness
around her seem to disappear. Lela is the author of *Knitting
Lessons: Tales from the Knitting Path* (Tarcher/Penguin, 2003)
and the editor of *Knitting Memories: Reflections on the Knitter's
Life* (Voyageur Press, 2006). Visit her at www.lelanargi.com to
find out about her latest writings and events.

The strange thing about memory is how reliant it is
upon external factors for its very existence. A pho-
tograph, a cataclysm, some twist of circumstance
will serve to lodge the smallest event in your mind with
great vividness, where perhaps more momentous details—
having received no such jolt or jog—are doomed to
languish in the perpetual shadow of id.

Aquarium Saturdays

After my father died, I found a trove of old slides in his desk that I had never seen before. For months I poured over them, enthralled, because they depicted certain phenomena of my childhood in a way that was completely surprising, causing me to reconsider and reorder my "memories." One showed me, at age three or so, wearing a kimono at a friend's birthday party. Incredibly, I had forgotten the kimono and the very dear woman who had brought it from Japan for me, a woman who played a central role in my mother's attempts to leave my father over the years, offering commiseration and refuge. She had given me the kimono at a particularly difficult time, as a small talisman of optimism and comfort. I had forgotten the kimono and all that it represented, even though I retained the *obi*—the decorative waist sash that came with the outfit—all the way through my junior year at college, when it eventually vanished.

I suppose the lesson in this is that what is lost can be found again, even if you didn't realize you'd lost something in the first place. As was the case recently when I was asked if I ever crocheted. My first response was an assured "no." And then, several minutes later, a complete reversal: "But wait…yes!" And with that dawning one wholly forgotten image of myself, very wet and sitting on the subway, crocheting something. The something, as it turned out,

Hooked

was irrelevant. For what I had dislodged from obscurity was not an old chestnut—an afghan or one of those ubiquitous 1970s patchwork vests or the first pot holder I ever stitched up for my mother—but a missing link, a piece of my own history.

This "new" memory of crocheting came, too, with a jolt. But I had probably been circling in on it for a while, only lacking the necessary focus to get me to it. The day the question came—I suppose I could also call it the day of the jolt—was a soaking one in central Vermont, where I had been living for just under a year. Unrelenting streams of water had been battering the landscape since before dawn. It had infiltrated my sleep and blurred my breakfast. Sheets of rain adhered to the window screens so that all views outward were hazy and surreal, like visions of the undersea when water has finally leaked in through your goggles. Since mid-morning I had been sitting at my desk, contemplating the rain and its ability to drive me inside myself, creating an atmosphere conducive to languorous thoughts and pleasant drifts of the mind. Rain was predicted for the entire week and weekend, and I wondered if Saturday would be a good day to take my daughter to the aquarium. And then I thought, as I had thought many times before, how funny it was that I only ever think to go to aquariums when it is raining. At the age of two, my daughter had been already on three aquarium visits—each time on decidedly sopping days. It was the same for me; my childhood was liberally sprinkled with wet, fishy Saturdays.

This was already in my mind when the crocheting question came. I had been thinking of one Aquarium Saturday in particular and its ceaseless gloom, and of how long a trip it must have been for my parents and me to get from our apartment on the very upper west side of Manhattan to the aquarium at the very bottom of Brooklyn. I was trying to puzzle out what series of subways we must have ridden to get there and back, and wondering how many hours it must have taken, and wondering what perverse strain running through my family causes us to always, only, seek out aquariums on rainy Saturdays. I had no memory of actually wandering through the aquarium this particular day, marveling at the sharks and rescued beluga whale I know resided there when I was in grade school. I remembered instead that I had chosen to wear my new sneakers—a pair of white, slip-on Keds I had picked out myself from a pile at a local discount store—over my red rain boots, which rubbed painfully against the backs of my calves. And how, when the sneakers became inevitably soaked in the downpour as we left the aquarium, they felt

Hooked

heavy as lead on my feet and oozed cold rainwater over my puckered toes with every step.

The crocheting question came, and I dismissed it, going back to my musing on that rainy Aquarium Saturday circa 1974. I saw myself sitting on the subway, on the way home and soaked to the bone, my parents sitting a few seats away, facing my profile. And then I saw that I was crocheting. I couldn't quite believe it at first, and I re-checked the memory to make sure I wasn't knitting or coloring or reading. But no, the memory was true, and suddenly I could see and feel white acrylic yarn between my fingers, and the cool metal hook as I looped it in and through, and my absolute engrossment in this act, forced at first and then actual, blocking out everything and everyone around me.

How on earth did I learn to crochet? I cannot for the life of me remember—not where, not who taught me, not when, although clearly it was sometime before I turned seven, my age on this particular Aquarium Saturday. It seems to have entered and exited my life quickly, although perhaps this memory is also inaccurate, a function of the fact that I maintain only this one image of myself crocheting and no other. However it came, and for whatever reason it went, though, it served a singular purpose in my young existence.

Aquarium Saturdays

Because here is what I can now tell you about that Aquarium Saturday and about our trip home on the subway that day. I have already said that I was soaking wet head to toe, and I was also wishing I were otherwise. I wasn't just cold and uncomfortable; I was uncomfortable in my own skin, embarrassed to be wet, my clothes sticking to me, my hair beginning to frizz. I know this sensation, remember it, because it has been reinforced so many times throughout my life: a swift opening of the sky and my impulse to run through the deluge. And then, my arrival somewhere—the inside of a shop or a subway car which is full of dry people who have sensibly used their umbrellas against the rain, and I am an outsider among them. Or the sudden about-face of the weather, from drenching to bright and sunny, the atmospheric shift abandoning me in obsolescence, my dripping condition senseless in the new context.

But I can glean this, too, from what I see of myself on the train on that particular Aquarium Saturday: I have spent the whole day with my parents and, drained by the experience, have chosen to sit apart from them. There has been fighting—always fighting with my parents; actually, less fighting than dangerous bullying by my father, and sullenness creeping in to infect our mood. Additionally, my father has recently had surgery to remove a cancerous

Hooked

vocal cord and part of his voice box, and has not—nor will he ever—regain his voice completely. He speaks in a harsh, loud grate that causes all who hear him to turn and stare. As is the nature of self-conscious seven-year-olds, I feel no empathy for his embarrassment about this, only my own mortification. I am this day, as I am every day that I spend with both my parents, or with just my father, pretending that I am elsewhere.

The crochet makes perfect sense in this climate of alienation and resentment. I can take it with me anywhere, and anywhere I need some form of escape, crochet provides it. This is why the outcome of my work is irrelevant; I am not crocheting to make a tangible thing, I am crocheting to transport myself. I am soaking wet, physically and emotionally discomfited, and also sure that the dry people around me on the subway are regarding my wet, frizzy state and finding it pitiable. Hook in, loop, and out; with this focus, I can steel my mind against my unease and paranoia. To my right, my mother broods and my father skulks malignantly. Hook, loop; hook, loop. My parents blur and I am alone, adrift in self-induced oblivion. Otherwise, without this distraction, I know that I will fade to my actual self, a small, hopeless girl drowning in a puddle of her own tears and despair. Strange that I should have remembered the wet and the aquarium and forgotten the crochet; as with the kimono in the slides, it is clearly the point of the whole story.

I am mindlessly looping along when a voice manifests from the left.

"Excuse me, young lady," it says, and I turn to meet it. The voice belongs to an elderly lady, elegant in a fur-trimmed coat and trim black hat, sitting beside her pleasantly smiling, also elderly and elegant, husband.

"I am so delighted to see you crocheting," says the woman. Her voice is thickly accented. "It reminds me so much of the work we used to do, when I was a little girl in France." Her husband nods mutely along, content to let his wife have her say.

"Ahhh, yes," she continues. "I am so happy to see you at this work. You have made me so happy, my dear!"

If I said anything in response to this brief monologue, I don't know what it was. Most likely, I muttered a quiet, "Thank you." But with the woman's words, I know that I felt myself no longer alienated from the world but vibrantly connected to it. Wet, frizzy, sullen, and with-drawn I may have been, but on this particular rainy Aquarium Saturday, I had managed, quite literally and without even trying, to stitch myself into the world.

Extreme Crochet:
Rare but Serious Side Effects

by Linda Permann

IN HER ESSAY "EXTREME CROCHET," writer Linda Permann faces a challenge unlike those laid out in the rest of the stories featured in this chapter: She is unable to crochet because of a repetitive stress injury. As she weens herself from her crochet addiction, Linda organizes her stash and tries to come up with things to do that won't remind her of crocheting—a challenge in itself.

Linda is a craft and decorating editor for *Adorn Magazine*. Her patterns have been published in *Jo-Ann Magazine*, *Cutting Edge*, and *Stitch 'n Bitch Crochet: The Happy Hooker*. She runs a little Web site, www.lindamade.com, and is currently trying to figure out how to crochet with her toes.

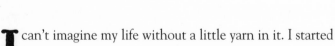

I can't imagine my life without a little yarn in it. I started crocheting steadily about four years ago when I moved to New York from Texas and needed a creative hobby that didn't take up too much space. I am largely self-taught, I continuously pick up things from parts of patterns or stitch dictionaries. There is always a new stitch combination, a sweater shape, or fancy yarn waiting for me to try. I imagine I could crochet every day for the rest of my life and still feel there were discoveries to make.

I remember one of my first questions: How do I hold the yarn? As in, what the heck do I do with my hands to get the proper tension? Luckily, not far into my experimentation, I ran into a woman named Rita on a bus trip to New Hampshire, and she showed me a clever wrapping technique (over the pinky, behind the index finger, then grasp the yarn with your thumb and index finger). It made things so much easier on my hands. When I took a free-form class a few years later, I noticed the teacher held her hook completely differently from me, sort of a like a pencil, hooking down into the work. I held my hook up, with a lot of twisting of the wrists. I crocheted this way for years, only once in a while running into some soreness if I went overboard. I had an administrative day job, so there was plenty of multitasking going on with my hands, and I frequently came home in the mood to work.

And then one day it happened. My dreams came true, and I was hired to research and design craft projects all day.

Hooked

I was in an office full of knitters, and there were freebies everywhere. I was a kid in a candy store of yarn confections.

I hoarded wool, collected handspun, and salvaged cashmere bits, cones of chenille, synthetic blends, and novelty yarns. I dyed my excess supply of bulky white wool. I invested in hooks and needles galore, and there were more to borrow from work if I ever needed a certain size. I had inspirations and patterns and experts at my fingertips. I tore out pages of magazines for crochet inspiration at work and put them into two folders—one for the magazine and one for myself.

I was always eager to come home, put the hook in my hand, and crochet away. I crocheted on my couch (repetition), stitched at concerts in the park, and knit while riding the subway to summer parties. I wasn't going to become one of those people who got to do what they loved for a living and stopped doing it at home, and I certainly wasn't going to start hating it. How could I not continue to crochet like the devil when there were virtually endless supplies? For the first time in my life, I had enough of the same yarn at one time to make larger projects—and it wasn't acrylic.

Of course I was anxious to try my hand at a few new things, and okay, maybe I went a little overboard. There were so many yarns to play with, each suited for different projects I'd dream up in my head. I crocheted pillows, hats, scarves, shrugs, pins, stuffed animals, belts, and chunky sweaters. I taught myself to knit. I showed off my projects and became friends with the yarn editor, who sometimes gave me great skeins before she put them in the giveaway box.

Sure, I had no place or need for some of the stuff I was making, but who does? I had new accessories to wear all the time. Single-skein wonders turned into hats and scarves I'd list in my online shop. I was proud of myself for using up my stash, and I was really enjoying all of the playing and discovery. Making stuff for other people meant I could go a little wild and not worry if it was something I personally would wear.

But about six months into the new job, I started to have pain in my right wrist, and eventually my left, too. First it was an overall feeling of swelling, something that I thought I could just shake out because I wasn't feeling it acutely anywhere. Then I started to notice a strange feeling near the pinky side of my wrist whenever I had to turn a doorknob. Typing became a problem, and my wrists felt a lot weaker than I was used to. I noticed it not only during needlework, but also while writing, carrying home groceries, washing the dishes, and even while washing my hair. I immediately worried that I had carpal tunnel syndrome—it's every crafter's nightmare, and it started to concern me, so I cut back. It didn't really make sense that it would kick in now, when I was doing much less typing than at my last job, so I brushed the notion aside. I started making little brooches from fabric, crocheted circles, buttons from my grandmother, and random bits. I figured they were small projects I could still complete without too much strain, and it became a fun texture-mixing experiment. But I couldn't sustain it once I realized grasping the needle to sew also irritated my wrists. Holding the tail end of the yarn hurt. Eventually, eating soup with a heavy spoon even started to bother me. I just couldn't believe that a little bit of harmless crochet could cause anything, especially not after four years, so I put off going to the doctor, hoping the aches would subside on their own while I wasn't doing any crafting at work.

I remember talking to a noncrocheting friend about it over lunch, and she suggested I just take a break for about a week, then go on vacation as planned, and by the time I came back I'd surely be better. I was incredulous—I couldn't just not crochet for two weeks! But it was worth a try, so I did end up putting a halt on my personal crochet projects for that week and during the vacation. It seemed to have some effect, but when I came back to New York, so did the pain. I finally went to the doctor, hoping he wouldn't laugh at me. But really, I was hoping he would. I desperately wanted to believe it was all in my head. He bent my wrists every which way, asked lots of questions, and announced that I had tendonitis, an overuse injury similar to carpal tunnel but much more treatable. Tendonitis—I could deal with tendonitis. It wasn't carpal tunnel, it wasn't permanent, and I thought that was great news.

"What kind of exercises can I do to help this heal?" I asked, imagining my excess time being taken up productively in a way that would help me get better faster. But he told me I wasn't allowed to do *any* exercises until I felt one hundred percent better. In fact, I had to cut back on everything, more than I already had. In his opinion, the cure for tendonitis was to do nothing—no crocheting, no crafting, no typing, no twisting jar lids or stirring cake batter. I even got out of emptying the trash.

He also prescribed some anti-inflammatory drugs as part of my "aggressive" treatment, given the nature of my work. The label made me do a double take. "May cause drowsiness" coupled with "Do not lie down for at least 30 minutes after taking this drug." The more daunting rare but serious side effects included "persistent stomach/abdominal pain, weakness in one side of the body, sudden

Hooked

vision changes, slurred speech" and my personal favorite "vomit that looks like coffee grounds." What? I thought I was helping my wrists here, and those sounded like some risks I didn't want to mess with. I took heart in the "Remember that your doctor has prescribed this medication because the benefit to you is greater than the risk of side effects" clause and took them anyway. If they were that rough on my body, they must work. Initially there was nausea, but if I ate a lot and stopped drinking alcohol completely, I was relatively safe. I just couldn't help thinking about all of the seemingly unrelated things I was giving up, things I hadn't thought of as choices before this.

When I came home I would stare at the yarn bins spilling over onto my living room floor. I could handle not crocheting, I thought, but not making anything? Not Web surfing? Doing nothing as a *solution*? I've never been good at doing nothing. If I sit in front of the TV, it's most likely because I want to crochet. If I was in the kitchen, it was to chop vegetables or cook a steak. If I was at my desk, I would be surfing the Web for new project inspiration. I had to forgo these things to sit in front of the TV—to *just* sit, and stare, and sometimes run the yarn through my fingers. I jotted down ideas for later and counted down the days till I'd have the hook in my hand again. I hoped the six months worth of refills I'd been prescribed was just generosity on my doctor's part, because he didn't make it seem like it would be a long ordeal.

Six weeks passed, and I wasn't feeling any significant improvement, so I scheduled another appointment. My doctor referred me to a hand surgeon for a diagnosis, but it would take three weeks to get in. I did some quick math in my head: three more weeks, plus however many weeks of physical therapy, plus more weeks of rest, I thought. So what did that make—twelve weeks till I could crochet again? I halfheartedly wished for someone to just smash my hands so I wouldn't be tempted to use them. The way I understood it, muscle inflammation was easy to build up, but hard to eradicate. Every time I made a move that felt like pain, I was taking a step backwards. I sometimes thought it would be much easier to absolutely not be able to do anything than to see if I couldn't just steal a stitch here and there. Tendonitis was a measure of my willpower, and I sometimes failed.

I was looking forward to my meeting with the hand surgeon, hoping my other doctor was right about him prescribing physical therapy. If I got to go to physical therapy I would be working towards healing, whereas currently I was working towards nothing and lots of it. Forced idleness produced the kind of anxiety that was traditionally what I'd work through with rhythmic stitches. This seemed like the universe's evil trick. It really made me wonder if this was what I was supposed to be doing with my life, and it enforced that yes, it was exactly what I wanted to do, even if it was a struggle.

While I was waiting for the hand surgeon appointment and wishing I had cable, I started to realize that it would still be a while till I got better. It had already *been* a while. I was sick of looking at my yarn, so I went through it. I pulled out all of the skeins I'd either already worked with or didn't foresee using. I took some of the yarn back to work and asked friends if they wanted the rest. The experience was freeing. It was my way of accepting that this would take time, that even when I recovered, I would have to cut back on my yarn affairs. Most importantly, I would have to be okay with that. I knew I wouldn't be using second-choice yarn any time soon, so I sent it to someone who would love it. I've been the recipient of two stashes in my crocheting past, and it's a special kind of challenge to work with someone else's choices. It was nice to give that back and realize that the cashmere carrot I was holding in front of my face to keep me going wasn't helping. I couldn't speed the healing process, it would simply take time. I've stopped collecting yarn at this point, but I still look down into the yarn giveaway box every time I pass by and I still have to touch whatever new fiber is currently sitting on the knitting girls' desks.

I went to the hand surgeon a few weeks ago, and he prescribed intensive physical therapy. It's been work to figure out where and how the problem movements are being made since I do so many different things with my hands. The doctor assured me tendonitis and carpal tunnel were nothing new and not always computer related—the first recorded case came from men deboning chickens in a factory. Still, that sounds a little bit tougher than crocheting too much, too often. I have to laugh a little when I go in for my appointments, three times a week. "Sports Therapy Clinic," the door reads. Who would have thought that yarn would lead me here?

I've been in physical therapy for about six weeks now, and although I'm definitely making progress towards reducing pain and giving my body the time to heal, I've realized that there will be no simple fix. My therapist has been wonderful in teaching me ways to incorporate my larger muscles into my routine to give my wrists a rest, but even if I play by all the rules, it may be another six months before I really feel "back." In the meantime, I am learning to crochet in small sections. Sometimes it is just a few rows at a time before I have to stop, and although it is frustrating, it's also taught me to slow down and think about my projects, and to really enjoy the work. My yarn is slowly making its way back out of the closet.

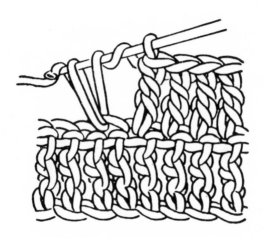

Crochet—The Gift I Finally Gave Myself

by Patricia Caliguire

DURING A PARTICULARLY LOW PERIOD IN HER LIFE, Patricia Caliguire turns to an old friend, crochet, to see her through. She finds the comfort she is seeking in the feel of the soft, warm yarn in her fingers and in the predictability of the pattern.

Patricia is a crochet designer/teacher and owner of Paanmo Designs (http://paanmodesigns.com). She is an associate professional member of the Crochet Guild of America and an affiliate member of The National NeedleArts Association. She lives with her family and many pets in Valrico, Florida.

"Accent Your Sewing with Crochet!" The words jumped off the page as I leafed through the fall issue of *McCall's* sewing pattern magazine. I had learned to sew and made all my own clothes, but I'd never thought about any other type of needlecraft. Crochet? Who crocheted? Certainly no one I knew did. In fact, my mother had been known to say, "We're not a very crafty bunch." But I was looking for a way to stretch my very small sum of babysitting money in order to buy Christmas presents for everyone on my list, and as I read the article I felt as if I'd struck gold. The article provided basic crochet instructions and included a pattern for a simple hat and scarf. I could do that, I told myself. Better yet, I could afford that.

Brimming with confidence, I hurried down to Woolworth's to pick up some yarn and a hook. I quickly located the yarn section and looked for our high school colors, black and orange, for my friends, and creamy white and beige variegated yarn for my mom and sister. I found a size H hook as called for in the pattern and practically skipped to the check-out counter; I couldn't wait to go home and start. To be on the safe side I picked up a booklet called *Learn to Crochet*, in case I needed help. Now I was ready.

Learning to crochet was easy for me, and I progressed rapidly. I tackled the hat pattern and made the first hat for myself in a very bright orange, wearing it proudly to school. Because I had been able to make the first hat quickly and finish it before the end of November, I knew I'd be able to complete all my gifts just in the nick of time for Christmas. Thus the crochet marathon began. I crocheted on the school bus, in the cafeteria, during Christmas-concert rehearsals, in study hall, sometimes even in class if I could sneak a few stitches in without getting caught. After making four hats, I started on three scarves. When I finally finished the last scarf, just before Christmas vacation, I thought with satisfaction that I now had a skill I could use for the rest of my life. Never again would I be unable to provide a gift for someone.

At that time, crochet was only a means to an end for me. Whenever a friend or family member needed to dress up their home or was expecting a baby, I had it covered. I crocheted fast, and for the next several years I crocheted for any and every occasion. While I appreciated the yarn colors and enjoyed working the stitches, the end result was all that really mattered for me.

In my mid-twenties I found myself crocheting less often. I had more money and less time, so I began to buy gifts instead. Once in awhile I would pick up a hook and a couple of skeins of yarn and work a few granny squares for an afghan, but they invariably ended up as dust catchers on a closet shelf, despite my good intentions. Other activities crowded in, and crochet took a back seat. My hooks were relegated to the depths of a dresser drawer and sank into obscurity. I added no more yarn to my stash, didn't set foot in a craft store, and thought of crochet, when I thought of it at all, as just something I used to do to save money. I had no need for crochet anymore—or so I thought.

Twenty years later my life took several unexpected turns. My father became ill and passed away, my husband lost his job twice when his companies were downsized, my mother suffered a hip fracture and needed my care. For a time there was little in life that was pleasurable at all. I felt as if I were merely going through the motions, doing only what needed to be done, just barely existing.

One particularly low day when my husband was headed out to the store, he asked if he could get me anything. I shook my head, but then reconsidered. "Wait— would you get me some yarn? Any kind, any color, I don't care, but just some yarn, please."

He looked at me quizzically, as I hadn't crocheted since before we were married, but he came back later with four skeins of soft, fuzzy baby yarn in pale pink, soft blue, sunny light yellow, and snowy white.

I didn't even know if I still had any crochet hooks around, but I rummaged through my sewing kit and found

Hooked

two ancient aluminum hooks. They were in the wrong sizes for the yarn I'd just received, but I could make them work.

The yarn colors were lovely, and as I touched them I felt a flicker of pleasure, the first hint of joy I'd felt for a long time. I had no baby to crochet for, nor did I know anyone with a baby; there wasn't enough yarn to complete a baby afghan anyway. But I started a simple ripple afghan design, thinking I could purchase more yarn and perhaps give the finished blanket to charity.

As my stitch increases and decreases formed ripples, I settled into a rhythm that I found comforting. Up, down, up, down, not unlike my life of late, but at least this pattern was predictable. I knew that after a certain number of stitches I'd reach a low point, but after a few more I'd be on the upswing again. Seeing the stitches laid out before me was heartening; I felt a growing sense of peace as I watched the sum of the stitches loop into a whole and beautiful piece of work.

When I came to the end of the yarn, the afghan was only two-thirds completed. As I had suspected, I'd have to go out to buy more yarn if I were to complete it for a gift. But for once this wasn't about what I was giving to someone else; it was about what I was giving to myself: pleasure and a sense of the order of things, a feeling of life itself actually making sense.

Crochet—The Gift I Finally Gave Myself

Instead of buying more yarn and finishing the afghan, I took the ripple afghan apart and enjoyed the yarn all over again, forming it into baby booties, into coasters, holding the strands together and forming the loops into hot pads and pot holders. I made swatches of clusters and popcorns, spikes and posts, all to give to no one but me.

When I had exhausted the yarn, and it began to look a bit ragged and more fuzzy than ever, I finally purchased more. I experienced that same pleasure every time I picked up a hook and threaded the yarn through my fingers to start a new project.

Over time I learned new stitches and techniques. I began designing my own crocheted items and patterns, and started sharing the enjoyment of crochet with others by crocheting blankets for charity and teaching the art of crochet. In fact, I found my life's work in crochet and now I have the privilege of designing and teaching crochet professionally.

Today my work in crochet almost always involves designing an item and pattern that I then give or sell to someone else. But I still keep the items I made, and even the scraps, from the yarn I used the day crochet pulled me back from an abyss of despair; I keep them to remind me of the day I began to feel alive again, the day I finally gave myself the gift of crochet.

Claiming Kinship: Finding My Way Home to Crochet

by Noreen Crone-Findlay

THE DEATH OF HER FATHER PROMPTS writer Noreen Crone-Findlay to take stock in her own life and appreciate the role crochet has played in making her the person she is today.

Noreen is passionate about the fiber arts. She is an author, designer, professional puppeteer, dollmaker, workshop facilitator, crocheter (and professional member of the Crochet Guild of America), spool knitter, small-loom weaver, and knitter. She is the author of three books: *Soul Mate Dolls: Dollmaking as a Healing Art*; *Storytelling with Dolls*; and *Creative Crocheted Dolls*. Over the past thirty years, her designs have appeared in many magazines, including *Interweave Knits*, *Vogue Knitting*, *Crochet*, and *Crochet Fantasy*. Noreen and her husband, Jim, make one-of-a-kind spool knitters. She writes a blog on spool knitting. Find it at http://www.lionbrand.com/archives/lbyarnblog7. Her Web site is www.crone-findlay.com

Claiming Kinship: Finding My Way Home to Crochet

Recently, my father died. My mother, siblings, friends, and I have been remembering stories about him and the times we all shared with him. Telling each other the stories is an important part of the journey through grief. It gives him back to us.

The death of my father made me look at my own life and gather the threads of my own story. One of the strongest threads in the tapestry of my life is certainly my connection to crochet. Crochet has been a powerful way of finding my way home to myself.

To begin at the very beginning, the story my father told of my birth was that when the nurse placed me in his arms, he looked at me and pronounced, "She's a gypsy changeling." He wasn't being unkind, he was just listening to the voice of his Irish parentage.

My mother's story about my birth is that I was born with knitting needles in one hand and a puppet in the other hand. (Ouch!) The gypsy changeling part of me showed itself early in my passionate love of puppetry. I did indeed become a professional puppeteer as an adult. And I cannot remember a time when I did not knit.

I didn't begin to crochet until I was eighteen. It was the early 1970s, and I was precariously navigating a rough

Hooked

passage. If people could be likened to yarn, then I was one tangled, messed-up skein.

In my first year of university, my parents had moved away precipitously and unexpectedly. I missed them and my baby brother terribly. I felt lost, bereft, and homeless.

I did not have a clue about who I was or how to create a workable life for myself. My "heart and head" passions were art and theater. My "heart and hand" passions were knitting, sewing, puppetry, and dollmaking. I did not yet know that these talents would be key to building my life.

My first two years of university were a soul-crushing time. I felt completely out of step with the painterly and sculptural approaches of the professors in the art department. There was blatant sexism towards the female students that left me feeling diminished and savaged. It was a disaster. I decided that I needed some time away to recover from the mindset of the academic art scene.

I still wanted to be part of the university community, so I got a job on campus. It was there that I discovered crochet—beautiful, magical, enchanting, healing crochet.

I worked with Tish Murphy, a splendiferous crochet marvel. Tish was a stunningly beautiful young woman who wore the most magical assortment of crocheted clothing.

Claiming Kinship: Finding My Way Home to Crochet

She had a wicked laugh and the sweetest, gentlest, most generous nature. She was a wonderful surrogate big sister. And she crocheted nonstop.

I watched her crochet, her hook flying, and went right out and bought myself a turquoise plastic crochet hook. I still have it. The price, ten cents, is emblazoned on it. Little did I know that I had just purchased the key that would unlock the doorway to a world of wonders and carry me home.

When I met Tish, I had been spewing out dresses, hats, sweaters, scarves, and shawls on a knitting machine I had bought with money I had earned after school. But when I fell in love with crochet, the poor knitting machine languished. It just couldn't hold a candle to my crochet hook. I sold it to feed my yarn habit.

Soon I was never without a hook. I churned out wild and fanciful garments, wall pieces, accessories, sculptures, toys, and dolls. I felt as if I were immersed in a glorious sea of color, texture, and shape. Before long, the crushing constrictions of art school faded away. Crocheting filled me with glee while healing my wounded heart.

I joined a cooperative gallery of kindred spirits and began selling my gypsy creations. The foundation of my life as a designer was built there, in that tiny gallery.

Hooked

My crochet hook became my paint brush, my sculpting tool, as I joyously crocheted wild, free, color-saturated, gypsy-spirited pieces. And when I began to explore the intricacies and mysteries of Irish lace, my crochet hook became my connection to my Irish ancestry.

My addiction to lace making had begun. The crocheting of Irish lace stirred me then and moves me still. It opened me up to a deep kinship with the women who created their masterpieces of lace in the darkest of times and kept their families alive with the flashing tip of the hook in the thread.

When I crochet, I feel a quiet contemplative connection that reaches back through time and across space. At the same time, I feel the wild exhilaration in the freedom of crochet. Crochet has the potential of being *anything*. It can be two dimensional or three. It can be a blazing uprising of colors and shapes or an intricate study of serene forms. Crochet, my beloved crochet: One loop on my hook and then another, filled with endless potential, endless promise, leading me forward, carrying me home.

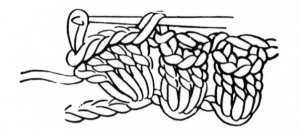

Chapter Four

THE ART OF CROCHET

The traditional tools, materials, and techniques of knitting and crochet inspire me in many ways. They carry with them many associations—of love and warmth, femininity and domesticity, comfort and healing, adornment and the body, culture and history, time and handwork in an age of technology. These associations can add a subliminal level of meaning to an artwork crafted stitch by stitch in fiber.

—Karen Searle, "The Art of Crochet," 2006

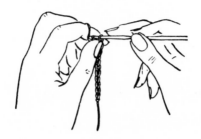

It's hard to believe that despite the surge in popularity in crochet and knitting over the past decade, both arts struggle to be taken seriously by the general population. Many would still scoff at the idea of displaying crocheted or knitted sculpture, sweaters, or panels in an art gallery. The stories collected in this chapter serve as proof that the art of crochet is very much alive, whether it be in the form of sculpture; crocheted shawls and sweaters inspired by ethnic textiles; or the vintage doilies, pot holders, aprons, and sweaters unearthed at garage sales and thrift shops that continue to inspire today's crocheters.

The Art of Crochet

by Karen Searle

KAREN SEARLE IS A FIBER ARTIST specializing in knit and crochet sculptural works. Her artworks have been exhibited in the United States and abroad since the late 1970s. She has presented classes, lectures, and seminars internationally, has curated fiber-art exhibitions, and served on international jury panels. She is a mentor to emerging artists through the mentor/protegee program of the Women's Art Registry of Minnesota. A former publisher of books on ethnic textiles, she writes about the arts for several publications.

I use knitting and crochet to create expressive sculptural artworks. By presenting a craft known for its functionality in a nonfunctional way, I am able to critique the generally accepted formal categories of conceptual art and decorative craft. The needle arts were not considered to be legitimate media for the art gallery until quite recently.

138

The Art of Crochet

During the 1960s and '70s the feminist art movement helped to legitimize "women's work" as both a medium for artistic expression and as a subject for art making. Since then, knitting, crochet, and other needle arts have been slowly gaining visibility in art galleries and museums.

The traditional tools, materials, and techniques of knitting and crochet inspire me in many ways. They carry with them many associations—of love and warmth, femininity and domesticity, comfort and healing, adornment and the body, culture and history, time and handwork in an age of technology. These associations can add a subliminal level of meaning to an artwork crafted stitch by stitch in fiber. In practicing these time-honored crafts, I feel linked to generations of women. I am using a quintessentially feminine art form to assert my own feminine viewpoint.

I use knitting and crochet interchangeably in my vessels, jewelry, sculptures, and installations, choosing one technique or the other for the nature of its stitch structure in order to construct my forms in wire and other stiff materials. Dense and firm crochet provides a solid base and lends a supporting strength; the open loops of knitting create light and airy or malleable areas. I have always thought of these two techniques as being complementary. In clothing design I enjoy the contrast of firm crochet bands on a soft knitted sweater, or the interplay of both textures in a freeform piece. In sculpture, I can take advantage of the contrast in structure and texture by juxtaposing constricted areas of crochet with billowy lace knitting.

Growing up in the 1950s, I developed an intense fascination with all forms of needlework, even though I had no role models for needlework within my family. I had heard that a love of needlework often skips a generation, passed on from grandmother to granddaughter. But I grew up grandmotherless, and the other women in the family used their creativity in different ways. (My mother's art form, for example was playing tournament bridge.) I never quite understood where my interest came from. I pursued it avidly though, going after all the home-arts badges in Girl Scouts, joining a 4-H club, and even looking forward to the sewing units during junior high school home economics classes. Knitting and crochet intrigued me, and I tried my hand at them several times by following the diagrams in an old "Learn How Book" that I had appropriated from my mother's mending basket.

I crocheted my first sweater the summer before I went off to college. I used granny squares, since I knew nothing about reading patterns at that point. The sixties had just arrived, and I proudly wore my creation as a badge of my

The Art of Crochet

individuality. My first roommate taught me to knit and to decipher a pattern (which I always had to change in some way), and my student job in a yarn shop honed my skills while aiding and abetting a growing fiber addiction. It also provided me with a yarn stash that carried me through my first few years of working as a civil servant. My fiber interest didn't wane, however. I worked out job frustrations by crocheting small swirls in red fingering wool that eventually became another pieced sweater. My high-fashion wardrobe of the time included a lace-knit cotton dress (very sexy) and a crocheted Chanel-style suit in a fine, dusty rose wool. Even though my body will never achieve a single-digit size again, both garments are carefully tucked away along with my wedding dress (which I seriously considered crocheting before resisting the impulse to add insanity to chaos).

During the seventies I took up weaving. That interest developed into a second career as I did weaving and knitting on commission and became an instructor at a local weaving school. Even then, crochet played an important adjunct role in my work as reinforcement, edging, or joining on woven garments and home-furnishing items.

I was nearly thirty when I discovered some details about the lives of my grandmothers that both astonished and elated me. My maternal grandmother had died when my mother was very young, causing her to live with relatives far from her birthplace. When she finally visited her home town in southern Illinois at age sixty, she met some of her maternal relatives for the first time and learned that her mother had been a weaver. Around the same time, my father, who had told us little of his early life, wrote and illustrated a memoir of his Chicago childhood for me and my sister. He grew up as the city grew from a small town with horse-and-buggy transportation into a bustling metropolis. In reading his memoir, I learned that his mother, who had died when I was four years old, had been a career woman who designed settings for a jeweler. (I also acquired some examples of her embroidered table linens and a crocheted afghan.) It was reassuring and inspiring to know that, in addition to tapping into a general collective feminine consciousness with my fiber work, I was also carrying on family traditions.

As a weaver, I discovered that I preferred to make one-of-a-kind items rather than do production work, and I focused on creating works of art. I also realized that my design sense is three-dimensional, and that, in addition to clothing, sculptural forms and figures most satisfy my creative impulses. I spent some time trying to force

The Art of Crochet

three-dimensional items from my loom before turning back to the familiar techniques of knitting and crochet in order to achieve contoured shaping effects with ease. Also, there is something greatly satisfying to me about creating an object out of a single, continuous thread, as opposed to the myriad of threads involved in weaving.

I began to make small doll sculptures using classic crochet materials that had been in use since the early twentieth century—small steel hooks and fine crochet cottons, the tools and techniques of my grandmothers' generation—to create works of deep personal expression. A series of small, rather plain, faceless people emerged, with openings that revealed brightly colored elements within. They could be viewed as portraying the inner secrets we try to hide and yet still reveal. Their presence affirmed my choice of fiber as an expressive art medium. In the nineties, after a thirty-year fiber-oriented career that included teaching, writing, and publishing, I enrolled in art school, crocheting my way to an MFA degree and pursuing yet another career as a fiber artist.

Today I work almost exclusively with crochet and knitting in a wide range of materials. Linen and wire are my current favorites, although I have tried just about everything from fishing line to hog gut. My sculptural forms and vessels deal primarily with the aging woman's body. A series of "Body Bags" (or portraits of women as bags) invites us to accept our sags and bulges with a sense of humor instead of the scalpel; a group of transparent-wire figures-within-figures suggests feminine strength and vulnerability. My work has traveled all over the United States and to several other countries, and sometimes I get to go along to give a lecture or workshop. Each day in the studio is an adventure. I can't think of a better way to spend my golden years.

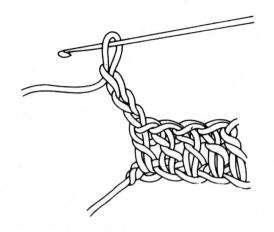

It's A String Thing

by Sheila F. Ruof

SHEILA RUOF, A PROFESSIONAL MEMBER of the Crochet Guild of America, crochets and writes from an artisans' village in the Sierra Madre mountains in Mexico. Sheila has been an investment banker, president of a Fortune 500 subsidiary, and principal of a management consulting firm. In her entrepreneurial life she served as president of four different start-up companies.

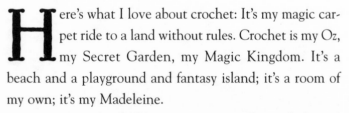

Here's what I love about crochet: It's my magic carpet ride to a land without rules. Crochet is my Oz, my Secret Garden, my Magic Kingdom. It's a beach and a playground and fantasy island; it's a room of my own; it's my Madeleine.

Let me just say up front: I am normally a rule-bound persona. In school I was the kid all the other kids could hate. The nuns at my Catholic school would offer a behavioral suggestion, and I would take it as primordially ordained. I kept my pen neatly on the right side of my desk, my posture ramrod straight, my feet squarely on the floor, and my eyes focused on the blackboard.

After school, I practiced piano with dedication. I earned the most badges in Girl Scouts. I was the babysitter of choice for the neighborhood. I read a book a day in the summer, just as my father instructed me. I was responsible, dutiful, earnest, clean, and kind.

But one passion could fuel my dreams of secret anarchy: crocheting. Other kids spent their allowance on candy; mine went for yarn, along with my babysitting money and the money I saved by walking home from school instead of taking the bus.

Saturday was the day to stoke my stash. We didn't have the luxury of yarn stores in my middle-sized town, but every department store and five-and-dime stocked yarns and crochet hooks, usually in the basement. My girlfriends would linger over costume jewelry and hair ornaments; I headed straight for the yarn. Some days I would longingly finger small ceramic dolls with hinged limbs, dreaming of crocheting them glorious miniature gowns. Other days I would splurge on a "jeweled" thread, not knowing what it would become, but enthralled by its endless possibilities.

147

Hooked

I built a collection of hooks, all metal, all so tiny the very thought chills me now. I unraveled sweaters for the yarn—decades after wartime rationing had ended. My mother and grandmother fed my addiction, pointing out things I could make, giving me their leftover yarn and baskets and boxes in which to store my stash.

I continued crocheting into my college years. And then, without notice, I stopped. You know how it is: early marriage, early kids, early career. All energy becomes focused on tomorrow. Before I knew it, I was a single parent and the sole breadwinner; the kids had tuition bills, and I was working longer hours.

Over the decades, other string things tempted me, like weaving and needlepoint in all its guises. I tried them, but I lost interest in every one, especially once computers got my attention. Computers reminded me a lot of looms: Both involve binary choices—follow the rules, and you'll be fine.

Eventually, I found some time for myself again. I consulted lists, composed over years of longing, for what I would do with free hours. I planned travels, I read—and I started to crochet again.

But this time it was such a different crochet! Where once I worked in miniature, now I chose fat hooks and thick yarns, or luscious mohair/angora/silky blends. Variegated yarns and hand-paints became my passion— until I saw a simple alpaca, loosely spun and draped in a skein.

As a young girl, I dressed small dolls in gowns, historical costumes, or fairy-tale fashions. Now I wanted to dress me, or women like me, in sensual clothes that speak of possibilities, of roads untried.

I create shawls based on a beautiful sunset. I use ethnic textiles collected over a lifetime as the basis for a garment or art piece. I love the whimsy of crochet. With just a flick of the hook, stitches can go backwards or forwards, around or on top, creating ruffles or tailoring, laces or loops. And I love crochet's flexibility. One week I'll start a lovingly reproduced traditional pattern, and the next I'll try to invent a way to use an unexpected fiber like liria or cactus to innovate with crochet.

These days I find that I am exploding with ideas for crochet. I tried keeping lists of things to make, but felt encumbered by the "have-to" expectation the lists placed on me. I do far better if I allow the spirit to move me, and if I create what I want to create this moment.

I've given up accepting commissions for my work. I make what I want. If someone likes it, she can buy it, but

Hooked

I won't make it again in another color; I won't make it again in a larger size. When I make things to other peoples' expectations, it begins feel like work.

Crochet has become, after all these years, my means to self-actualization. The act of crocheting is a sensual experience for me, and it is a life-affirming testament for others who see it. Their comments may be simple: "Why, you're an artist!" or "How did you think of that?" But what they're really saying is "Oh. You've helped me to see in a different way, and I see *you* in a different way because of your work."

My crochet is about creating. It has no rules, no restrictions. My string and hook can keep my secrets or unveil my dreams. My crochet can speak of far away shores, or reminisce about people I love. My crochet often precedes me, and I hope it will linger in memories of me. Crochet isn't just what I do. It's who I am.

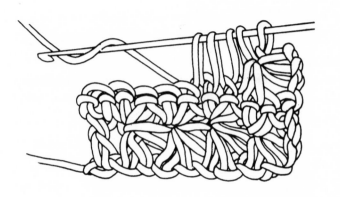

Weird Crochet

by Sigrid Arnott

SIGRID ARNOTT, A RECOVERING ARCHAEOLOGIST living in
Minneapolis, gets her husband and two sons to do all sorts of
crafty things with her. She figures that with all the money she
saves by thrifting she can indulge her love of all things to do
with fiber.

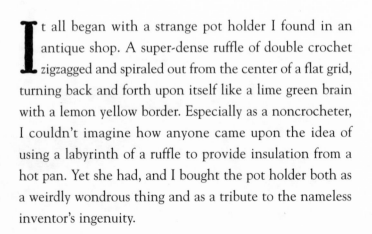

I t all began with a strange pot holder I found in an
antique shop. A super-dense ruffle of double crochet
zigzagged and spiraled out from the center of a flat grid,
turning back and forth upon itself like a lime green brain
with a lemon yellow border. Especially as a noncrocheter,
I couldn't imagine how anyone came upon the idea of
using a labyrinth of a ruffle to provide insulation from a
hot pan. Yet she had, and I bought the pot holder both as
a weirdly wondrous thing and as a tribute to the nameless
inventor's ingenuity.

Weird Crochet

Soon I had a few of these pot holders, and even though I couldn't puzzle out how they were made, the heft of the pieces and the myriad tiny stitches they held told me it had taken a fair amount of time to create each one. To go with my pot holders I found a table mat at a garage sale. Thirteen metal bottle caps were encased in foil, covered with radiating rows of variegated purple thread, and linked together to form a bunch of grapes topped by a bright green leaf. I loved the multi-media aspect of this creation; the way the soft cotton contrasted with the metallic heft.

My interest piqued by these bizarre creations, I began to search for more weird crochet. I had worked for some time as an archaeologist, digging though the garbage of the past and trying to "decode" the patterns of our ancestors' cast-offs. Now I found myself sifting through household rejects—those things that people want to free themselves from, yet feel deserve better than the trash. It used to be that I would study aerial photos then drive a Land Rover through the countryside stopping where the geography suggested ancient settlements once stood. Now I trained my eye to recognize garage sales advertised in the spidery handwriting of ladies in their seventies and eighties and then cruised my car to those houses where the exterior landscaping indicated doilies might be uncovered within.

· Hooked

I began to frequent the "bins" section of my local thrift store, where crochet abounds. Layer by layer I excavated place mats and hankies hoping to find hidden hot pads. Although I practiced restraint, I did collect such items as a lacey, yet weighty, variegated pink "hostess apron," a clothespin holder, and a mesh purse similar to an onion bag, but adorned with lace. All of the objects have in common happy color schemes, interesting construction, and the inability to properly perform their intended function.

Rather than construct quasi-scientific archaeological analysis of the "artifact" assemblage, I felt free to imagine possible scenarios in which my little things had been made or used. I pictured a rather dumpy Midwestern housewife crocheting away, mentally transforming herself into a pin-up worthy dame in high heels with the rosy lace apron hanging precariously from a ribbon tie. The clothespin holder was, I decided, a flashy bridal shower present that was "too good" to be left out in the weather and ended up preserved at the bottom of a linen closet.

No doubt that the variegated gold, pink, red, and green purse once held some child's treasures, perhaps some doll clothes and a yo-yo. I just can't imagine a grown woman having an ensemble it could have coordinated with, and the holes would not have contained the sorts of things that settle to the bottom of purses.

Sometimes, if the seller knew the creator, I could collect a little oral history to provide context for my finds. Often as I would dig through a stack of crochet items at a yard sale I would be told something like this: "My mother just loves to crochet. Why, she just crochets away every day. We all have a tablecloth (there are six of us siblings), and the grandchildren (all eighteen) have afghans, but she just keeps making these pot holders. I just don't know what to do with them all!" Then I would feel a compulsion to rescue some odd crochet item just so it wouldn't be unceremoniously toted off to the Goodwill with some ratty T-shirts.

Doilies rule the world of vintage crochet, strongly asserting the right for arcane geometrical patterns to merge with utterly useless household tchotchke. Circular crocheted objects, whose distinct stitches radiate out like a mandala from a central circle, held a mysterious appeal to me. The more functionally useless and geometrically elaborate, the more I was intrigued. I felt overwhelmed by the masses of circular creations that seemed to represent womankind's challenge to answer the riddle of pi in never-ending cotton lace. It seemed odd to me that so many women could say they are no good at math when they could create a perfect flat circle, or hexagon, or octagon, in lace pattern, no less.

Lace is a way of suspending holes within a stable fabric. So making a doily means a person creates pleasing, repeating geometrical patterns with these holes, while at the same time making the number of stitches increase by pi (or 3.14+) every time the diameter of the doily increases a by the height of the average stitch's width. (I think, but I am not very good at math. My favorite doily shows that the ratio of the circumference of a circle in relation to its diameter could also be solved by means of brightly colored pansies.)

Some ladies even went beyond pi, their hyper increases creating ruffling hyperbolae as they neared the edges of their doily. Who knows, it may some day be discovered that these lacey creations accurately describe the distortion of the space-time continuum at the edge of the universe or some other theory of physics. Some of the things I found are perfectly executed, but don't lie flat or are odd three-dimensional forms. These seemed to me to represent the testing of a hypotheses regarding three-dimensional spatial relationships. I came to believe that the little old ladies who made them were a lot smarter than they let on.

Weird Crochet

Sadly, I felt there occurred a decline in crochet sometime in the late 1950s and early 1960s. All of a sudden crochet items seem to have exploded in size while becoming hugely simplified in structure. Instead of intricate thread dresser scarves in delicate solids, one finds driveway-sized afghans in simple stitches and rioting colors. Lightning bolts of carrot orange and cosmos pink flash across fields of army green, or stripes of burgundy march next to contrasting bands of lemon yellow and tomato red.

My archaeology training sometimes overcomes me, forcing me to consider these changes in "material culture as a gendered dialectical response to transformations in society." (In other words, I wonder what inspired women to make new stuff.) If I were a true social scientist, I would have created hypotheses involving dietary distress and the concomitant loss of esoteric doily knowledge with the death of elders, or the oppression of female secret crochet societies by the rise of patriarchal hunting groups. As a sister crafter, I'm guessing that the shift occurred when the women started watching TV (instead of listening to radio?) while crocheting. Having to keep one's eyes *off* your work required bigger stitches, brighter colors, and simpler patterns. At the same time, synthetics came on the market, and there was a profusion of thick, bright, inexpensive acrylic yarn perfect for the new crocheting technique. There was probably also the problem that every surface in every crocheter's house except the couch was already provided with a crocheted doily.

I puzzled over the fact that from the needles of knitters came sweaters and mitts, but crochet seemed to spawn household oddities or fantastical afghans. All those scores of stitches and creativity ran amok (or so it seemed to me). Instead of creating something useful, a warm garment, for example, crocheters seem bent on creating dust-catching doilies and covers for inanimate objects that don't need to stay warm, such as wine bottles or rolls of toilet paper. Instead of focusing on creating a thing of beauty to be a joy forever, crocheters seemed to prefer to create a thing, a strange thing to be a puzzle forever after.

I suppose I should come clean and admit that my interest in crochet was closeted—literally and figuratively. To be honest, my decorating style doesn't go well with doilies and toilet-tank covers, and most of my discoveries ended up in a box in my closet. Worse, I am a knitter, and for some reason those who knit are, as a tribe, snobbishly anticrochet. Finally, most archaeologists I know would find me insane if I admitted that I would just as soon dig through a bin at a local thrift store as go catch a mysterious disease while excavating an Inca tomb in South America.

Then *I* learned to crochet.

Or rather I relearned, overcoming a decades-long block I had developed as a child who couldn't make a granny square.

Crochet has it over knitting in several ways, I found. It is faster to make and way easier to fix. Best of all, after years of knitting, which requires hours of calculations before one can cast on and finally settle into actually stitching, I felt wildly liberated to make one loop and just spin off from there. Let me explain that, as a knitter I can't follow directions and I like to be creative, but my knitting is quite conventional. I make sweaters, mittens, and scarves using natural fibers in what I hope are tasteful colors.

But my crochet . . . it's weird. In just a little over a year with this craft, everything I have made started from a circle and grew outward. Nothing is rectangular unless I connect motifs; there are no sleeves or necklines, and I tend to favor strong (or are they just odd?) color combinations. When people see my knitting projects they say, "Oh, pretty!" or "I wish I could knit." When they see my crochet projects they say, "*In*-teresting . . ." or "My aunt, the one who had fifteen cats, she used to crochet . . . ."

Hooked

First I made hats in single crochet. After increasing out, I just stitched down until the hat fit someone. I used bits and pieces of yarn from my stash, so the hats have wild green stripes that don't match any clothes of anyone in my family. Yet they are worn.

Ponchos were big, and the gift-giving season loomed, so next I made a necklace-sized chain from which I spun a niece-sized acrylic blue web that ended in a trendy blue-green boa yarn. The niece's best friend commissioned a companion piece that I made in yellow with a sun-burst border. They weren't beautiful per se, but they were loved.

Then a friend gave me some vintage rayon crochet cordé in aqua, pink, and cream. The twists and turns of my hook with this shinny stuff made crochet that looked like upholstery braid or some expensive trim. I decided it would make a perfect 1910s style drawstring purse—a reticule to dangle from one's wrist. Too bad I ran out of cord before I reached the top. I decided to wash and block it anyway while I figured out how to finish the project. After I squeezed out the water, I searched for an appropriately sized thing to dry it on and found that a full roll of toilet paper was just the thing. As soon as I finished arranging my creation upside down upon the roll and stretching out the lacey edging, it became obvious. I had created a spare toilet paper roll cover!

I had to laugh because for years I had scorned those voluminous crocheted skirts cascading off a Barbie torso and over a spare roll of toilet paper. Now *I* was the unwitting designer of a roll cover, and, truth be told, it was just the thing for for hiding such necessities in my 1920s aqua bathroom with no vanity.

Next I went into granny-square overdrive. The granny-square obsession began innocently enough, as I wanted to overcome my block with this particular motif. After cautiously and carefully completing the granny square that broke the spell, I found how fun it is to improvise on the simple rules that make this motif grow from a tiny circle of yarn.

First I made a shoulder bag in fall colors. Then summer vacation rolled around. I had two loud boys, ages five and eleven, in close proximity to my person 24/7. I knew I needed some strategies for mental-health management, thus "granny-square time" evolved. Once or twice a day I announced it was time for me to make a granny square and then went to the porch to do my "job." It was understood that mothering duties were on a slow down during the time needed to make a square, and that should I be

Hooked

overly bothered by unnecessary demands, there was some risk of an outright strike on my part. (One great thing about my kids is that they accept some of my eccentricities without question.)

I had picked up some fine singles yarn in six shades of red, orange, and green and a hook whose size, as far as I could tell, was simply "10¢." With just these colors and a few rules about which colors could be next to one another, I began to improvise on the four-row granny square. How satisfying it was to actually complete another unique square and pat it into shape feeling as if I had just done something of significance. The pile grew, my yarn supply dwindled, and I thought only of the next square.

"What are you making?" my husband politely asked one day as he joined me on the porch.

"Granny squares," I answered with equanimity, although thinking it was pretty obvious what I was up to.

"I guess . . . I mean . . . what are you going to *make?*"

"More squares. I haven't even tried starting with dark green or ending with lime, but then I have only made about forty . . . ." I babbled on about my work, my favorite color combinations, as though I were a great composer who had not yet finished exploring the musical variations upon a simple melody.

Weird Crochet

Now he was practically bursting. "But are you going to put them together, make some *thing* out of them?"

"I'm not crocheting any *thing*," I retorted with irritation, "I'm just crocheting."

"Oh," he said, and we both pondered my pronouncement.

I realized I hadn't felt the need to make something useful or even beautiful, such as an article of clothing. I hadn't felt the need to do anything beyond play my little color-combination game, row by row and square by square. I sat, letting my hands do their part while my mind unwound itself like the little skeins of yarn that grew softer and springier as I pulled the twists and tangles from their centers. I was finally getting closer to understanding the motivation of my sisterhood of crocheters who had made the pot holders and doilies in my collection.

Now fall has arrived, and the boys are back to school. I'm ready to complete some big project, ready to "make something" with the sixty-plus squares sitting in their basket. There are too few for a wild afghan, but I've been thinking I could make a crib blanket, or a really long scarf, or a gypsy-granny skirt, or a bunch of pillows, or a toaster cover, or a kitty-cat tent, or a microwave cozy. I have thought about sewing them in cubes, stuffing them and making ten lucky granny-square dice. Or I could sew six nine-patch squares into one large cube. Really, the possibilities are endless.

One thing I know for sure, someday when my creation ends up in a thrift store somewhere, someone will pick it up and exclaim, "Look at *this* weird crochet!"

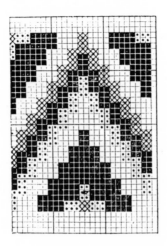

Thrift Store Crocheter

by Jennifer Hansen

JENNIFER HANSEN IS THE FOUNDER and chief creative force behind Stitch Diva Studios (www.stitchdiva.com), a company that specializes in innovative knit and crochet patterns. A professional member of the Crochet Guild of America, her fresh perspective on knitting and crochet has been featured in various online publications, books, and magazines, including *Vogue Knitting* and *Interweave Crochet*.

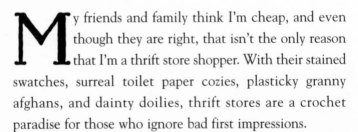

My friends and family think I'm cheap, and even though they are right, that isn't the only reason that I'm a thrift store shopper. With their stained swatches, surreal toilet paper cozies, plasticky granny afghans, and dainty doilies, thrift stores are a crochet paradise for those who ignore bad first impressions.

Granted, I was a thrift store shopper long before I ever picked up a crochet hook. I do have high-minded friends who are drawn to thrift store shopping as the ultimate act of recycling and reuse, but my attraction to thrift stores has always been much more visceral and self-minded. It is the hunt for the deal: It's the $175 Nambe serving platter I found for a steal at $5, the antique Turkish Kilim I found for $20, or my set of four vintage Trader Vic Tiki mugs, purchased at $3 (now used to store my knitting needles). And beyond the thrill of the hunt, it is the spirit of exploration and discovery: I buy things that I'm only marginally interested in because the price is right—like the two-dollar yogurt maker because I wanted to try to make my own. I made yogurt for a few weeks with my new appliance, discovered it was easier to just make in the oven, and after a few months decided it wasn't worth the hassle to make it from scratch at all. I donated the yogurt maker back to the thrift store and learned a new life skill for a very small price. I would have never experimented in the first place if I'd had to pay retail.

My obsession with crochet, however, has given my thrift store expeditions new meaning, starting with the obvious enticements of new kinds of deals. There are the tool deals: At a fraction of retail, it has been affordable to build up my crochet-hook collection to include every size I can find. And I've found more than just the run-of-the-mill aluminum hooks: I've found old bone hooks, handmade

Hooked

wooden hooks, casein hooks—collectible hooks with character. Because the price was right, I've bought crochet tools I didn't know how to use: those funny crochet hooks with the hooks on both sides, those long crochet hooks with a stopper on one end, and those funky hairpin frames. Having these unusual tools in my possession challenged me to research and learn how to use them. When I work with these old hooks, it is comforting to think of them long ago in someone else's hands, creating a family heirloom or something of meaning in that person's life, and that now the hook has found new purpose in helping me with my own work.

There are the yarn deals. The stashing behavior of the typical crocheter is a standing inside joke. We all amass way more than we will use in our lifetimes, and these stashes find themselves on the shelves of thrift stores when we destash or die. Sure there's lots of cheapo old seventies scratchy acrylic (perfect if you want some low-cost supplies for your experiments, such as microwave felting), but there are also wonderful discontinued yarns with charming, old yellowed labels—premium yarns that I might not typically allow myself to purchase without a specific project in mind. I once found an entire garbage bag of hand-dyed wools, some in hanks and some already hand-wound, for four dollars. They became the materials for my first forays into felting.

And then there are the deals on pattern magazines, leaflets, and books. How else did I learn to use my hairpin-lace loom and my Tunisian crochet hooks but from old yellowed books value-priced at fifty cents? Through my thrift store finds, I discovered that my very favorite crochet publications are from the seventies. For me they are windows to the minds and souls of a flower-child era and a period of great innovation in the craft. My crochet library is dominated by out-of-print works with super-funky photography and styling. I couldn't buy these items brand new even if I wanted to, and I wouldn't have discovered them if I hadn't been a thrift store shopper.

But the real treasures are the cast-offs that other people have already crocheted. For me, the only thing that is more fun than browsing for inspiration through a new crochet pattern book or stitch dictionary is browsing through raw, real-life crochet work. Real people's work that I can touch and view from any angle—wrong side, right side, close up—picking apart the stitches with my fingers to absorb the work with all of my senses. Uncensored crochet work by unsung designers, not work that has been specially selected for my consumption by a book or magazine editor and then relegated to a one-angled, untouchable photo-graphic image. Like a crochet archeologist, I find swatches used by anonymous crocheters to prove out their own innovations, and I find half-completed projects from another era that are thrown into bags of half-used yarn. I find entire completed projects: old pot holders, blankets, tablecloths, dish towels, pillowcases with crochet edgings, granny-square blankets, bottle-top pot holders, stained doilies, and crochet-edged aprons. I find ponchos, shawls, jackets, and baby layettes. Each project I find, no matter how abused, no matter how ugly the yarn or colors, has a little story to tell me. Some stories are old hat, some are very familiar but presented with a new twist, and once in a while I find something that is truly a lesson for me: a hair-pin-lace join I haven't seen before, a doily-stitch combo that would make an excellent inset for a skirt, or that fas-cinating three-dimensional pot holder I found that I'm still not really able to qualify or accurately describe. I've got a storage chest of crocheted items at home, filled with these little nuggets of inspiration.

I know it sounds like a joke for me to say that thrift stores have taught me how to crochet. But for a "modern" gal like me, who never learned the craft from my mother, grandmother, or aunt, it has been thrift stores that have provided the most continuous and intimate crochet instruction. I read somewhere that before the written crochet pattern existed, stores that sold yarn and threads would have samplers of swatches that they would make available to their customers; crocheters would "read" the actual samples in the same way that we read patterns today. It reassures me to know that even if this practice is no longer routine, the thrift store ensures that it is still around in a very real and grassroots kind of way that will probably never disappear. Thrift stores are serendipitous purveyors of the crochet craft; they exist in almost every town, provide free access to quality crochet artifacts, and even offer them for purchase on a budget. The adventurous need only look past stains, wear, and blemishes for a most unique, intimate, and unadulterated source of crochet inspiration and instruction.

Chapter Five

CROCHET IN THE SPOTLIGHT

There are three times more crocheters in the U.S. than knitters, and crocheters use a third more yarn than knitters.

—Craft Yarn Council of America

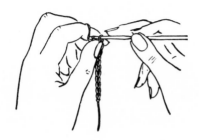

There's no doubt about it, crochet is hot! Crochet is everywhere these days. Crocheted cardigans and pullovers adorn fashion-conscious women and girls. The knitting club that gathers at my local coffee shop on Wednesday nights once consisted of only knitters, but now just as many of the women crochet. And catalogs for popular women's clothing stores feature more crocheted sweaters, tunics, scarves, and belts than ever before. Crochet has definitely found its place in the spotlight, as the stories that follow confirm.

Confessions of a Poster Child for the Yarn Industry

by Lily Chin

LILY CHIN BEEN KNITTING for more than thirty-five years, designing for about twenty-five years, and teaching for more than fifteen years. She has written several books, including *Knit and Crochet with Beads*, published by Interweave Knits; *The Urban Knitter*, published by Berkley Books; and *Mosaic Magic—Afghans Made Easy*, published by Oxmoor House. Lily is most proud to be the first American designer to have her name on a yarn label. The Lily Chin Signature Collection of yarns and patterns debuted mid-2005; to view the yarns, go to www.lilychinsignaturecollection.com. Lily also has a new TV show in the works. The pilot for Stitchcraft, her new show on knitting and crocheting, is debuting on the Oxygen Network in spring 2006.

Lily has been a "poster child" for the yarn crafts for the past decade, specializing in sound bites and putting forth a good face for knitters and crocheters at large. She has appeared in dozens of newspapers and on scores of television shows, including the *Late Show with David Letterman*. In the following essay, she provides a glimpse into how it all began.

Confessions of a Poster Child for the Yarn Industry

"**H**ere's some gift-giving advice this Christmas. Don't knit, grandmas knit, and after years of receiving misshapen sweaters and toaster cozies, the world is sick of knitting." This was from a national radio ad. It went on. "Get something useful instead (from Sears), like a telephone or a computer or a fax machine."

Imagine my chagrin upon hearing this back in December of 1991. Although it specifically targeted knitting, I've heard many similar things said of crochet. In this particular instance, a northeastern yarn company had alerted me to it. I tuned in to my local all-news station here in my native New York City. "Do something about this," the yarn company implored.

One has to remember that there was a time, not so long ago, when knitting and crocheting were not the hip, cool hobbies that they are today. Many, if not most, will recall that these crafts were considered relics, anomalies, representatives of a bygone era.

Why did the yarn company choose to contact me? What made them think I could "do something" about this ad? Alas, there was a painful modicum of truth to the stereotypes. The yarn crafts had indeed been populated by participants of more advanced years. Being twenty-something at the time made me stand out. Then there was reputation and personality. I was known then (and still am, no doubt) to be bubbly, outgoing, and even rather outrageous. I also, immodest as it will seem, was deemed a "babe." Wearing risqué outfits like midriff-baring halter tops and super-short mini-skirts was the norm for me. Add to this the fact that I was an accomplished knitter and crocheter of renown already plus a resident of one of the most major, if not the biggest, media centers in the country. All in all, I represented a potent package. The combination of these characteristics made me a good candidate for industry spokesperson.

Thus began my journey as the poster child for the yarn crafts. I was put forth as the prime antithesis of the stereotype. The industry trotted me out when trying to dispel that dowdy image of knitting and crocheting.

Mind you, I never thought there was anything bad in that image. I actually like the warm, cozy connotations of grandma. Let's face it, though. It's just not sexy in the media. Sex sells. Besides, what I really object to is just plain ol' stereotyping, period.

So how did I counter the radio ad? What was my approach? I staged a public protest, a showing, really. I gathered glamorous grannies and men and children who knitted and crocheted. I put in a call-to-arms to members of our Big Apple Knitting Guild (no small feat during the holiday season). We stood outside a local Sears store with our crochet and knitting projects in hand. We got newspaper coverage, all right—a full page in the *New York Daily News* via a reporter who, coincidentally, was also a member of our Big Apple Knitting Guild. A photographer snapped a large photo of me in a gold lamé gown that I'd knitted and crocheted, with a slit up to the hip bone and a backless, plunging keyhole. It was good, old-fashioned cheesecake. They called our protest a knit in rather than a sit in.

Truth be told, this time was not a very good one for the yarn crafts. Yarn shops were dropping like flies, yarn companies were closing their doors, yarns and accessories got more and more difficult to find. The chain stores saw no need to carry yarn at all. The old mainstay, Woolworth's, folded. In order for the hobbies to survive, they needed to be sold to a new generation, to appeal to new blood. We needed new converts to up the numbers and make the yarn industry viable and healthy again. A healthy yarn economy means yarn shops prosper, which means more choices for knitters and crocheters: more patterns, more books, more magazines, more tools, more yarns.

Hooked

It was at this point that I made it my personal mission to do whatever it takes to make knitting and crocheting more visible and more attractive. I was and still am a designer for the industry, so portraying knitting and crocheting in a positive light also directly affected my livelihood. In order to have demand for what I offered, there had to be more knitters and crocheters.

On the personal level, I tried to knit and crochet in public whenever and wherever possible. I figured if more people saw someone stitching, it might put the idea into their heads to give it a try. It might just pique enough curiosity and interest. Or there may be lapsed knitters and crocheters who, upon seeing someone doing it, might have that desire rekindled. Thus, I worked on the subways, at the theater, in the park, wherever.

Comments were often disparaging and discouraging: "When are you expecting?" "I didn't know people still did this kind of thing." "You're too young to be doing this." "Haven't you better things to do with your time?" I had snappy and prepared comebacks, as I came to expect such put-downs: "I'm expecting you to leave me alone." "You're obviously too ignorant and untalented yourself to be doing this." "I'm doing something constructive with my time, what do you have to show for yours?"

Confessions of a Poster Child for the Yarn Industry

I began to kick it up a notch. Teaching at national conventions and knitting/crocheting shows meant "yarning" on planes and hotel lobbies. In the process, I started to gain more publicity. Every time an article on knitting or crocheting was featured, reporters sought me out for comments and interviews. There was the Gannett chain of newspapers, the *New York Times*, CNN, local news stories. Again, I was the token person representing the new face of the craft.

Then around the middle of the 1990s, something began to happen. Interest began to rise. Yarn crafts were coming to the forefront, and with the increased popularity yarn came more publicity, more interviews, more "mugging" for the cameras. The Craft Yarn Council held its first Knit Out and Crochet Too in 1998. Stories about knitting and crocheting celebrities such as Madonna and Julia Roberts started to appear in magazines. In January 2000, *Time* magazine quoted me about the hot, trendy things to do called knitting and crocheting.

I began to write books to fill the demand. My first book, *Mosaic Magic—Afghans Made Easy*, was a crochet book released December 1999. My second book, *The Urban Knitter*, featured knitters across the country (both men and women), each representing a major city, each in their twenties or thirties. The book came out February 2002.

With the books came book tours and publicists who got me on local media. I started to show up in newspapers and television shows and radio programs on a fairly regular basis, about once a month. The feeding frenzy was on. As the yarn crafts took off, so too did word of them. Invariably, the "angle" of the news stories was how the traditional crafts are gaining a renaissance as more and more young people take it up. The other hook was how knitting and crocheting have become the new yoga, as they are a great and productive way to relax in our stressful world. The celebrity angle was usually included in the mix as well. I'd become quite expert at giving the pithy sound bites, those twenty-five-words-or-less answers to those invariable questions. Reporter asks: "Why are knitting and crocheting so popular today?" My reply: "They're so relaxing, they call them the new yoga. Besides, the celebrities who are doing it have made it trendy. What better way to express your creativity and multitask in a productive way?" To me, I sounded like a broken record. Alas, it was what the reporters wanted, what they expected to hear. I just had to keep making it sound fresh every time I said it and tried to keep a straight face.

Confessions of a Poster Child for the Yarn Industry

Then in October 2002, the Craft Yarn Council of America, in conjunction with the British Handknitting Confederation, came up with the mother of all publicity stunts. In searching for the fastest knitter and fastest crocheter in the world, they held local competitions in each country, then pitted the best in the United States against the best from the United Kingdom. I'd competed in almost all the regional competitions in America and had a showdown with the woman from the United Kingdom, Susan Briscoe, at the Knit Out and Crochet Too event in New York City.

To say that this publicity stunt worked would be an understatement. What I loved most was that little ticker-tape ribbon on the bottom of CNN News. That day, it read: " . . . Sniper strikes again in Maryland, bombing in Kuwait, Lily Chin is World's Fastest Crocheter . . . ." There I was, right up there with the other international disasters. Reuters news-wire service picked it up, so the story appeared in newspapers across the country.

Next thing I knew, I was asked to crochet a sweater for David Letterman on CBS's *Late Show* in May of 2003. Then came a whole new round of media coverage, as my third book, *Knit and Crochet with Beads*, was released in February of 2004. From spots on national television shows

Hooked

the CBS's *Early Show* and *Martha Stewart Living* to the local news shows in Atlanta and Dallas to cable networks like ESPN and MSNBC, I'd made more than fifty appearances in about two years. I give my time freely and gladly. It usually entails getting up in the wee hours of three or four o'clock in the morning in some strange city. I have to put on full makeup and do my own hair, no small task—it takes about forty-five minutes. I then usually have to take a cab while it's still dark to some remote and/or industrial part of town where the news station is. More often than not, I perform like a circus seal or a trained organ-grinder's monkey. The usual format has me begin a project at the top of the news hour, then they show my progress intermittently throughout the show. Towards the end of the broadcast, they'd interview me and show my completed project, usually a scarf or shawl (though I did a football jersey on ESPN and a poncho for a chow dog on *Martha Stewart Living*). I am usually toting loads of projects, a mid-sized suitcase's worth, for display as well. Having crocheted for about an hour, sometimes two, I'd then tote all my things back to the hotel and begin a full day of teaching or do a local book signing. It is grueling, not glamorous.

In October 2004, I'd successfully defended my fastest-crocheter title in London against the same woman from

Confessions of a Poster Child for the Yarn Industry

England. I don't take my title as the fastest crocheter in the world all that seriously. I know that the real *raison d'etre* was to gain visibility for the yarn crafts. I just do my duty and talk up crocheting as much as I can. What tickled me the most was the opportunity to present crocheting to a general audience. I'd done crafts shows on the *Do It Yourself* (DIY) Network and *Home and Garden Television* (HGTV). To me, this was preaching to the choir. I wanted to introduce crochet to a more general audience, one filled with potential knitters and crocheters who have not given the crafts much thought before.

I don't think of myself as being so important as to bear any direct responsibility for this renaissance in now-trendy knitting and crocheting. I'd just like to think I had a slight hand in it—a hand that brandishes a hook or a needle. My new moniker: our lady of perpetual publicity.

...But Is There an "Ebb" Stitch?

by Gwen Blakley Kinsler

GWEN BLAKLEY KINSLER, founder of the Crochet Guild of America, feels her talents lie in her ability to reach crocheters and unite them to sing the praises of the craft. A widely published author of articles on needlework and patterns of her crochet designs, she is co-author of *Jumbo Book of Crafts* (Kids Can Press, 2005). Although she has led the campaign to banish the granny image of crochet for over a decade, Gwen is in awe of our foremother's skills and inspired to make what is old new again.

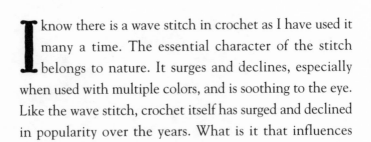

I know there is a wave stitch in crochet as I have used it many a time. The essential character of the stitch belongs to nature. It surges and declines, especially when used with multiple colors, and is soothing to the eye. Like the wave stitch, crochet itself has surged and declined in popularity over the years. What is it that influences those waves or ebbs and does it matter? I have been consistently passionate about crochet since 1971 and have no intention of losing that passion. To me, crochet is soothing, it pleases the eye, it gives satisfaction and a sense of pride upon completion—and besides, my crochet to-do list is way too long to stop now. I am content in the knowledge that crochet is more than just a chic trend for me, and I will continue to love the craft even if this wave peaks and its popularity declines.

Over the past decade, I have personally experienced the wave that has brought the popularity of crochet to an all-time high: it's hot, it's cool, it's hip, it's in. More crocheters have become part of my universe, as have more patterns and yarn choices. I am thrilled that more and more crocheters have discovered the same joy I have found in crochet. I loved crochet when it was not popular and I crocheted alone. But like anything, there is satisfaction in the camaraderie of others who enjoy the same activities. I longed to be a part of a community of crocheters, but found none.

Back when I started crocheting in the 1970s, I wasn't really in the closet with my crochet because I took it to work and furiously crocheted each day during lunch hour. But I certainly didn't tout it or offer to teach it to anyone.

Hooked

Crochet didn't come up as a topic of conversation, and I wasn't forthcoming with my pride in the process. My quiet pleasure with crochet was no less then than it is now. I thought it didn't matter to me that I was the only crocheter for miles around, yet there was a nagging sense of wanting to connect.

During the next decade, I had children, and as a young mother I gravitated toward others with kids the same age. Lucky for me, my neighbor friends were quilters, and we shared our stitching joys. Our dynamic friendships and passion for our various crafts led us to promote ourselves and others by producing craft fairs. When my one-of-a-kind creations sold, subtly the concept of pride in my crochet work began to develop.

Now, with a stronger need to learn and join, I became a member of the local embroiderer's guild, as there was no crochet guild at the time. Learning to embroider and being around other creative people was satisfying, but crochet was always by my side. During the guild business meetings, I would crochet as unobtrusively as possible so as not to offend others. I haunted yarn shops and met many other crafters, but crocheters were hard to find in my close-knit group. I was the only crocheter in the embroidery guild, and I felt like the only crocheter for miles around.

...But Is There an "Ebb" Stitch?

From sports to opera, there are superstars that carry the torch and encourage others to join in. Not so with crochet. In 1986, I came upon a *Chicago*-magazine clipping of an artful hand-crocheted purse covered in buttons. This feature, my first crochet sighting, gave crochet the prestige it deserved and me the validation I needed. Between 1986 and 1997, I continued to collect crochet sightings in the media: movie stars at a premieres wearing crochet; a model in an ad for an unrelated product, like Splenda, dressed in crochet; a department store selling a crocheted purse. Like the spaces in filet crochet, there is a gap in my collection between that first clipping in 1986 and 1993 when my crochet-sightings crusade began in earnest. From 1993 until 1997, I was able to fill only one three-ring binder. During that time, however, crochet came into sync with the direction of fashion. Writers often described crochet as making the leap from its traditional, stale granny image to a way to create hip, sexy clothing. And, because the clothes were typically handcrafted, they had an appealing human touch as well. For the younger fashionistas, what was old had become new. The granny square was revived and lace work was in fashion. Journalists using play on words made it appealing: "Open season, Granny's crochet makes a sexy comeback" (*Chicago Tribune*, May 12, 1993).

Hooked

Moschino Couture showed a granny-square skirt ($915) and matching tank ($810) (*Chicago Tribune*, April 10, 1994). A crocheted mohair top was on the cover of *Cosmopolitan* magazine (February 1996).

A particularly good year for crochet fashion sightings was 1997: Linda Dano wore a crochet hat in an article promoting her book, *Looking Great...It Doesn't Have to Hurt* (*TV Guide*, March 29, 1997). In a Loréal makeup ad, the model was wearing crochet (*Elle*, April 1997). "In Stiches: Granny had it going on. All those handmade caps, scarves, and gloves she crafted with care are the inspiration for this season's hottest cool weather looks" (*Woman's Wear Daily*, April 1997). The year closed out with crochet on the cover of *Teen* magazine's prom issue (December 1997). Most visible were the SAK ads, which artfully displayed their crochet bags several times a year.

In the early 1990s, a ring of crochet friends began to encircle me. It was a combination of luck, determination, and yearning that hooked us together, and we formed a group that would become known as the Crochet Guild of America (CGOA). It was a complete thrill for me to find that I, an unknown entity, could create and offer a weekend of crochet classes and other related activities in which ninety strangers, who love crochet as much I do, would participate.

...But Is There an "Ebb" Stitch?

Since 1994, the CGOA has used crochet sightings as one of the many ways to forge new links and recruit new guild members. Participating in both trade and consumer shows, we desperately wanted to battle the stereotype that crochet is just for grannies. We used the crochet-sightings file to educate others about crochet—its beauty, variety, and versatility. More often than not, knit-shop owners who turned their noses up at the mention of crochet changed their attitude after seeing the many celebrities fashionably dressed in crochet. Those clippings were inspiration for guild newsletter articles, promoting design ideas and reassuring new members that we are not alone in knowing the wonderful potential of crochet.

It wasn't long before my new crochet friends learned of my growing obsession with collecting media sightings about crochet. Soon I had a growing chain of "cro-sighting agents" from my local chapter of the CGOA and from around the country, who began clipping and sending crochet-related articles and advertisements from magazines and newspapers.

During 1998, crochet slip-stitched from fashion runways to accessorizing stars and to ready-to-wear catalogs. Crochet sightings proliferated, and we've collected enough ads and articles to fill a binder each year since. One highlight from that year was Madonna appearing on the cover of the July 9–23 issue of *Rolling Stone* magazine wearing a gold-lamé crocheted gown.

The year 1999 was one of self-expression. A November 26 *Los Angeles Times* article said, "Being able to cast off sweaters and dresses lovingly made by moms and grand moms for mass-produced clothes was once a symbol of improving family fortunes. Today the handmade look is hip. It's a symptom of the backlash against futurism and technology. Not that we are turning to sewing, but this generation has found a new skill: looking like no one else!" On the brink of the new millennium, Grandma's craft found new appeal. In April of 2000, the *Chicago Tribune* said, "Women who came of age in the sixties when crochet was too much like what grandma did for free, were asking, 'Why can't I be a woman of power and still be creative?'" In 2001, Oscar de la Renta expressed the look of the moment with his crocheted camisole that sold for $1600. The appeal of crochet then was its ability to reveal and to conceal (*Vogue*, July 2001).

Beyoncé wound in the new year by wearing a lacy crochet halter top to the 2002 Teen Choice Awards, and many stars were now in the loop, wearing crocheted garments or actually enjoying crochet's relaxing benefits

...But Is There an "Ebb" Stitch?

between takes backstage. "We yearn for yarn and companionship in a world of uncertainty," said *USA Weekend* (April 2002). *Elle, Cosmo, Glamour*, and *Lucky* were a few of the many magazines that featured cover models dressed in crochet garments that year.

With "Stitch 'n Bitch" groups clustering in coffee shops, bookstores, and yarn shops across America, crocheters and knitters became sister stitchers in 2003, as many knitters became interested in learning how to crochet.

Through crochet, new yarns in vibrant colors and interesting textures found their way to college campuses as students became hooked on the craft. Even guys found a common thread and began to crochet. One student expressed the thrill: "Magically, once again magic, because I don't understand how it works, but you get this fabric out of a ball of string" (*Texas Tech University Daily*, March 2004). In early 2005, when Martha Stewart admitted in the March issue of *Elle* magazine that she used crochet as a way to relax while in prison, the popularity of our beloved craft soared.

American Girl Dolls Inc. brought crochet into the consciousness of thousands and thousands of potential new crocheters when they introduced their "Girl of the Year 2005," who just happened to be wearing a crocheted hat,

Hooked

scarf, and necklace. Later that year, when Martha Stewart walked out of prison wearing a crocheted poncho, crafters and fashionistas alike busted their bobbles trying to find a pattern to make one themselves. It seemed as if everyone had to have that poncho.

At that same time *Elle* magazine explained, "Crochet is experiencing a renaissance, appearing on everything from handbags and gloves to jaunty sundresses. While certain types may enroll in crochet class, most haute-hippies will be satisfied to sit back and admire the handwork of our favorite designer. Isn't that what modern luxury is all about?" (*Elle*, March 2005)

My term on the board of directors of the CGOA has ended now, but I don't know if I will ever be able to stop collecting crochet sightings. It is still a thrill to find them. The year 2006 started off right with Madonna on the cover of *Elle* magazine wearing a crocheted skull cap (February 2006). In an article about the Juicy line of clothing going couture, writer Kevin West describes a crocheted dress, the first look designed in the current collection, "You could wear it with flip-flops at a hotel resort or wear it New Year's Eve with a Diamante bag. It's very LA." (*W* magazine, February 2006)

Is this wave of crochet about to peak and crash as some naysayers believe? I don't know, but if so, I will invent the

...But Is There an "Ebb" Stitch?

ebb stitch and enjoy the ride until the next wave. It was more than a decade ago that my dream of a crochet guild began to grow, one row at a time. I never dreamed that I would become an author, designer, and teacher of crochet, my passion. Crochet sightings have been a meaningful part of my fabulous journey. My hope is that the many new crocheters will learn to love the process along with the project and their interest and satisfaction will always be at peak levels, ensuring yet another generation of crocheters.

Coming Home to Crochet

by Dora Ohrenstein

EVER WONDER WHAT IT WOULD BE LIKE to be an up-and-coming professional crochet designer? In her essay "Coming Home to Crochet," Dora Ohrenstein provides a glimpse into that face-paced world.

Dora is a professional singer who was vocal soloist of the Philip Glass Ensemble for ten years. She has more than twenty commercial recordings to her credit and teaches singing at the college level. She specializes in crochet fashion, and her designs have been published in several recent books and magazines.

The passing down of "womanly arts" formed no part of my childhood experience; I did not learn cooking, sewing, or any needlecraft from my mother. None of the women in my family had any interest in such things. My mother's mother, a bourgeois lady in the city of Antwerp, Belgium, had maids in the house, as was typical at that time and place. Instead, I was encouraged to be musical, and I was; eventually I became a professional singer and voice teacher, and that's how I've made my living for a long time.

But before my musical career began, I was part of that rebellious generation of the 1960s that proclaimed the Age of Aquarius as a glorious new dawn. In 1970 I quit a prestigious college and ran off to points around the globe, seeking fellow free spirits. My parents were, of course, mad with worry. I eventually settled in the city of Amsterdam, where I purchased a tiny houseboat for one hundred dollars and lived in it for about eight months. Along with the notorious questionable practices of my fellow Aquarians, about which I remain mum, there were also positive forces that drove the hippie community. Motivated by a wish to "get back to the land," people eschewed commercial products and learned to make things themselves. As a result, the 1970s saw an explosion of creativity, which affected crochet no less than any other craft. The art of crochet took many fabulous forms: remarkable clothing, works of sculpture, masks, and other "far out" pieces that defied definition altogether.

In Amsterdam, I met a young Scandinavian woman who was a weaver, with her own shop not far from my little boat. The place was enchanting, with giant cones of richly colored yarns neatly arranged everywhere. My friend gave me some samples and suggested I take up crochet. I learned some basic stitches from a book, and not knowing how little I knew, started making clothes simply by holding swatches up against my body and adding stitches where more fabric seemed needed. I remember my very first project—a skirt and matching cape in brilliant orange, teal, and yellow stripes (we hippies were not modest about color). The canal where my boat was parked was near a street of fancy boutiques. I brought my handiwork to a woman's clothing shop and offered it for sale. They liked it, hung it in the window, and it sold within a few days. So did the next two projects I made: a dress and a motif vest.

Although I was very pleased with my success, I didn't make much of it at the time. Not long after, my parents caught up with me, and ultimately I realized I had to return to a "normal" life. I went back to school and became a singer and citizen of the real world. In all the years when I was involved with music I never thought about crochet and never had a skein of yarn or hook in the house. Life was too full and demanding to think of such things.

Then two years ago, during a summer when my work life was slow, I suddenly had the urge to explore the craft

Coming Home to Crochet

again. It was like getting back on a bike after many years—I simply took up where I'd left off, using the same ad hoc construction methods as before. I studied some patterns, but never could work from them: As soon as I had a swatch of any size, it would beg to mutate into something other than what it was meant to be. So once again, I stood at the mirror, turning and moving the work this way and that, figuring out ways to grow it into the idea for the garment that was floating around in my head.

I never thought of this as designing, but I did get all the pleasure and satisfaction of creating. And my new crochet clothes—vests, jackets, skirts, sweaters, and summer tops—looked pretty nice, according to my fashion-conscious Manhattan friends. In the summer of 2004, I decided to go to a Crochet Guild of America (CGOA) conference in Manchester, New Hampshire, anticipating opportunities to upgrade my skills, meet some pros in the field, and commune with other hobbyists.

On my first day, I was awaiting the arrival of classmates and teacher in the chilly, overly air-conditioned room. A woman with white hair whose face radiated intelligence and good humor walked in and sat down next to me. She complimented me on my crocheted top, a cotton, short-sleeved, striped peasant blouse. She asked if I had created

Hooked

the design myself, and I said yes. She asked if I had ever thought of making money with crochet. I told her I had, but given the hours it took to make a garment, how could one ever charge enough to make it worthwhile? Well, said my companion, you don't sell the garment, you sell the design to a publisher. The dear woman then revealed that she was in fact an editor of pattern books and was seeking designs herself. What else did I have, and could I come by with the garments that evening to show her and her partner?

So began my relationship with two of the leading figures in knitwear publishing, Jean Leinhauser and Rita Weiss. Jean was founder of the American School of Needlework (ASN) and Leisure Arts. Rita worked for many years as an editor for Dover, an important needlework publisher. They had been working together at ASN for many years, and when that company was sold, they founded Creative Partners, an entity through which they create books on an array of needlework crafts for top publishers in the field. That evening I brought several tops, sweaters, and a coat to their hotel room, and they purchased six of my designs.

As a newcomer, I could not have been more fortunate in my first venture into the business. Rita and Jean know everything there is to know about the needlework industry, and they are thoroughly professional about payments, contracts, and deadlines. Furthermore, they are the most delightful women—strong, independent, funny, and great mentors.

At the same conference I befriended several other up-and-coming designers—Doris Chan, Vashti Braha, Tammy Hildebrand—and we traded stories eagerly. It was a very exciting time; crochet was clearly having a renaissance, and we were thrilled to be part of it. I also met Kathleen Powers Johnson, an established designer and teacher, who haw become an important mentor. Kathleen is remarkably generous in sharing her expertise, and I still call her regularly for encouragement and advice.

The December following my first meeting with Jean, she invited me to visit her in San Diego. We spent a delightful week, and I was permitted to browse her enormous library of needlework books and magazines. At one point Jean, who spends much of her time editing patterns, was lamenting the imprecise pattern writing of some designers: "You've got your hook, and you need to know exactly where to stick it!" she said. This hilarious phrase inspired the following ditty I wrote later that day, meant to be chanted, a la hip hop, to a loud, obnoxious rhythm track:

Stick It

A pattern isn't good if it has any ambiguity
If it isn't clear, use your ingenuity
When you have a problem, there's a way to lick it,
And when you've got a hook, you gotta know where to
stick it.

CHORUS:
Stick it, stick it!
You gotta know where to stick it, stick it!
I know from experience 'cause I'm no fool
A girl's got to know what to do with her tool.

The hook is an instrument of grace and power.
I like to play with it hour after hour.
But when I'm following instructions, it's really very wicked
When they don't tell you just exactly where to stick it.

CHORUS:
Stick it, stick it!
You gotta know where to stick it, stick it!

Coming Home to Crochet

I know from experience cause I'm no fool
A girl's got to know what to do with her tool.

So boys, if you wanna join the crochet rage
Better make your swatch, better check your gauge
Have hook, can travel, if you've got the ticket
All you need to know is exactly where to stick it.

CHORUS:
Stick it, stick it!
You gotta know where to stick, stick it
I know from experience cause I'm no fool
A boy's gotta know what to do with his tool!

OVER THE NEXT MONTHS I struggled to master pattern
writing and attempted to understand sizing. It was a sink-
or-swim situation, and at times I felt overwhelmed. I had to
redo two of my designs for Jean and Rita in different yarns,
which entailed substantial redesigning. The more I
learned, the more I realized how little I knew. Jean taught
me how to write instructions. Kathy helped me take on the
daunting challenge of planning a garment—including all

Hooked

the sizes—in advance. For those who haven't worked this way, it can require days and days of math, especially in my case because I like shaped garments, complex stitch patterns, and color changes. Writing instructions for such complicated patterns can be a nightmare. The realities of being in the business have definitely given me a different perspective.

My new profession had to be worked around my day job as a voice teacher at two different colleges. Often I would take projects along on my commute to work and crochet on the subway, train, or Staten Island ferry. Through crochet, I was able to make extra cash while enjoying a great creative outlet. Crochet was also a calming force in my noisy, stress-induced urban life. My practice was to come home after an eight-lesson day, nuke up some tasty morsels from the local upscale market, then settle down with some yarn, maybe a glass of wine, some jazz on the radio. After a while my mind would be purring on a totally different plain. Time would pass without my awareness—I'd look up and it would be two a.m.

This past summer I attended my second CGOA conference in Oakland, California. It was wonderful to realize I was almost a somebody in the crochet world—a very minor somebody whose name and work was becoming recognizable to editors. I sold several designs during the conference and made excellent contacts for future projects. My crochet buddies from the year before all had great tales to tell and lovely designs to coo over.

Unfortunately, the conference was overshadowed by a looming deadline, and I ended up spending a good part of the time holed up in my room finishing a dress that was behind schedule. Deadlines are, of course, an ever present, nagging concern for the published designer. Plan as one might, it is not uncommon to run into a snag with your concept, yarn, or execution and find yourself in a panic, begging for an extension.

And there are other challenges to designers, such as figuring out what publishers want, keeping up with the trends, and creating swatches of the proposed design. Publishers will, from time to time, send designers a request for submissions, which outlines the styles and fashions they are seeking and invites designers to make a proposal by a certain deadline. Most often they want something terribly chic that is also very easy to make and not too costly in yarn. The designer's proposal consists of a swatch—a crocheted sample showing the stitches, colors, and some of the shaping, plus a sketch of the finished piece. Such requests for submissions are sent at unpredictable intervals, but the deadline is never too far away. In fact, it's often close enough to make you, the designer, feel hard pressed to find the yarns, dream up the concepts, and create a swatch that will successfully sell your idea to the publisher.

And then there's math. I rather like math. I also like the idea of planning the entire garment beforehand. But because I often use unusual construction, I must also devise unique calculation methods: Do I need to measure here or there? Does this measurement need to be divided into halves or quarters. And although I'm not a total nincompoop, I don't have any real talent for math and often make mistakes. Keep in mind that the designer must plan the garment in four sizes. Further, that crochet-stitch patterns, especially in the fashionably bulky yarns, are clunky, by which I mean they can measure as large as two or three stitches per inch. This in turn makes fine-tuning a beautifully shaped armhole or curved neckline a daunting task, one that has defeated many a brave designer. I have had more than one experience like the following.

A very desirable publication purchased one of my swatches for a long cardigan/coat. They wanted the same stitch pattern, a complex one, but in a very fuzzy yarn where it couldn't possibly be seen. They wanted it in a plus size, but could not supply enough yarn, as the yarn was

Coming Home to Crochet

brand new and simply not available. And they wanted it in ten days. I tore out a lot of hair and bit my fingernails shamefully. I devised a clever solution to the lack of yarn of which I was quite proud—I cut away the front edges of the garment on both sides, which ended up being quite flattering for the plus-size person. I spent two days figuring out the math so I could do a set-in sleeve in this very clunky stitch pattern. For those who have not attempted such a thing, the goal is to create a nice curve from the bustline, up the armhole to the shoulder, losing the correct number of inches so you end up with the proper width across the shoulders. Then you need to make the top of your sleeve, or sleeve cap, match and fit perfectly into this armhole. I tested my math with several large swatches to make sure it would work. I submitted the finished design and waited months for it to come out. When it did, the pattern had been changed to a drop sleeve, no armhole, no sleeve cap. I can only say—expletive deleted.

As in any new endeavor, there's always a learning curve, and challenges are to be expected. But the truth is, this incident and several others were beginning to rob me of the pleasure I took in the craft. My swatching came to a halt. I looked with indifference at new yarns. My collection of inspirational books lay dormant on the shelves.

Hooked

I began to question my choices. Was I meant to be in the design business? Was I making merely commercial projects rather than those I really want to make? Did I do better work when I was designing for myself and friends? Was I enjoying the craft more before I learned how to do all the math and preplanning? I'm still asking these questions, still wondering whether I can locate that marvelous intersection called the best of both worlds.

Lately I find myself browsing again in the inspirational books from which I've learned so much: Dettrrick's *Design Crochet*, Jacqueline Henderson's *Woman's Day Book of Designer Crochet*, Sally Harding's *Crochet Sweater Book*, and Sylvia Cosh's *Crochet Style*. These designers did such fine work; somehow they were able to balance innovative design without ever talking down to their audience. After paging through the books, I know I still want to make beautiful things and there's so much more I want to learn and try. And I also know that I do want to be part of this community of people who share ideas and create inspiring designs for publication.

I'm convinced that the high-quality work featured now in crochet publications is a sure sign that this craft is not going underground any time soon. There's an energy afoot that's bound to lead in new directions, create new audiences and outlooks, and afford new opportunities for designers. I'm fortunate to be able to step back and take another look at what I really can and want to do, and I'm grateful for the extraordinarily good breaks that have come my way.

Did I mention that I live in a one-room apartment? It's got my bed/futon, dining table and four chairs, microwave, desk with computer and printer, bookcases, dressers, filing cabinet, couch and end tables, refrigerator (because I don't have a real kitchen either), and, oh, an upright piano. Can you imagine what it's like, in such circumstances, to store your yarn stash and actually be able to find what you need when you need it? Every nook and cranny—and there are lots of those in this pre-war building—is filled with baskets, trunks, and boxes, each jam-packed with yarn, beads, buttons, and other crafting paraphernalia. It's now at the point, and I am not exaggerating, where I cannot buy a single item, be it a DVD, new piece of clothing, or (shudder) skein of yarn without throwing something else out.

What I've decided to do, during my mid-semester break, is to create some space in my little Manhattan home—I will make bucketloads of small garments to sell retail. There's a flea market every Sunday in a school yard right across the street from where I live. A couple of knitters

Hooked

and crocheters seem to be doing very well there. The chic shops along Columbus Avenue have beautiful crocheted hats and scarves at ridiculously high prices, too. For these small items I intend to make, I want to mix up lots of different yarns in playful ways. I probably won't end up making so very many, but if I can at least come up with some prototype designs for hats, bags, and scarves, I'll be pleased. I've emptied out all the baskets and boxes, and there are skeins strewn all about the couches, tables, dressers, the piano bench, and a few on the floor. I'm going to tell people I'm away so I don't have to pick up the phone or answer e-mail. I've got several of my favorite books open to remind myself of special techniques I want to try. This is starting to feel like fun again!

A Life with Crochet

by Lana Bennett

IN "A LIFE WITH CROCHET," writer Lana Bennett tells the compelling story of how crochet leapt in and out of her life before she found her true calling meeting and interviewing the most revered crocheters in the industry.

Lana describes herself as a bit of a "Jane of all trades" who found refuge and beauty in crochet. She was born to conservative Midwesterners in the culturally and geographically diverse setting of Southern California, just after World War II. She spent the first half of her life playing the piano and discovering her own values, tastes, and preferences and deciding where she fit in this complex world; she has spent the second half getting there.

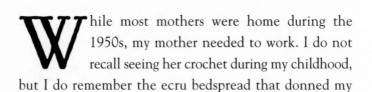

While most mothers were home during the 1950s, my mother needed to work. I do not recall seeing her crochet during my childhood, but I do remember the ecru bedspread that donned my parent's bed. I had been told my mother, my grandmother, and great-aunt had made the coverlet. It was made of squares with stand-up spirals and popcorn stitches, and it was lovely.

One of my older sisters, Pat, on the other hand, crocheted during her every spare minute. Pat was much older than me, and she married when I was only four. She and her husband and my parents soon purchased houses, side by side, in the then small town of Gardena, California.

On every available surface all over her home, Pat placed crocheted doilies. Big, round things, stiff as boards but intricate in design and often done in the popular pineapple motif, became the platform for all manner of milk-glass candy dishes and knickknacks that were also in vogue in the 1950s. On any summer afternoon, when my niece and nephews were napping, I might find my sister with either crochet hook and thread in hand or placing drinking glasses between starched segments of newly finished doilies in order to cause them to dry in stiffened ruffles. Honestly, I was never all that impressed with the doily frou frou; consequently, I did not have a desire to crochet myself at that time. But the memory of my sister's efforts, when I look back, was meaningful to me and planted a seed to be harvested in my future.

Hooked

On occasion, my maternal grandmother would visit. Grandma Bingham was very old fashioned to my developing, West Coast eyes, with her long, homemade dresses and black, two-inch heeled shoes that laced. I loved my grandmother. She had time to spend with me that my mother did not have, and she did things like bake bread and make tea in the afternoon. And Grandmother was always working on something. If it was not a crocheted runner or doily, it was an embroidered one. Today it is her crochet work that I treasure the most. Fond of filet crochet, she left a trunk load of filet throws, doilies, arm-rest covers, and tablecloths.

Up until the early 1960s, most of the crochet I had been exposed to was made of white or ecru thread, although I had seen my sister crochet with stiff, wool yarn, and in 1966 she made me a sweater of orange acrylic that I relished. Among the many cultural shifts that came swiftly into all of our lives during this era was a renaissance in needlework. Crochet was suddenly showing up in the fashion and Bohemian worlds in bright colors, flamboyant styles, and in stitches and yarns I had not seen before. This was when I became truly interested in crochet, but I was unable to do anything about it right away. The Vietnam War had started by this time; I was married to my high-school sweetheart, and we had a baby. My husband was drafted, and I had to find employment. Tragically, more than two years later he returned changed and unstable, and we soon separated.

It was in 1971, and after moving from California to the Midwest, that I purchased a crochet-pattern booklet for a beach cover-up and finally picked up a crochet hook myself. The ankle-length cover-up had three-quarter-length sleeves and was made of sunny yellow, acrylic granny squares. I bought the yarn and the hook and, with determination as my only strength, taught myself to crochet according to the directions that were provided. This first project became a gift to my former roommate, who still lived in California. No doubt it had many flaws, but to me, it was gorgeous, and I was very proud of my gift. As I continued to crochet, I became familiar with the designer Annie Potter and her well-known "Annie's Attic Catalog," which she had started out of her home. Annie's use of color and her somewhat whimsical patterns often brought to mind the color and flowers I had left behind in my home state of California.

From that point forward, I took advantage of any creative opportunity that came along. I learned to weave and purchased a large floor loom; macraméd lampshades, plant and bookshelf holders; sewed men's ties and vests; and

Hooked

made all sorts of interesting garments in bold colors, complete with patchwork, bell sleeves, bell bottoms, and bell inserts in jeans. My son, Michael, who was a rather shy, introverted child, enjoyed drawing and assembling plastic models, but above all else, he loved the story of Peter Pan. He asked me to make him "sword-fighting" shirts, which I did with abandon, using leather laces and jeans with fabric inserts to match the shirts and I crocheted. By this time, I found that I liked doilies that were not starched, and I discovered crocheted lace techniques in addition to filet crochet, such as broomstick lace.

Soon after, while I was attending the University of Illinois in Chicago and taking Latin American studies, biology, and Portuguese in hopes of getting a degree in nursing with minors in language and minority studies. I was also working as a staff member in the in-house student quarters for the middle and high-school–aged children of adults who were living outside the country and working as community developers. I set up a crafts center for the students that had all manner of inviting things to do: candle making, lap-loom weaving, drawing, collage, and of course, crochet. Many crocheted scarves came of this endeavor, and one of the boys wove a beautiful family seal in addition to the long, blue scarf he crocheted for himself.

A Life With Crochet

During the 1970s, some women were beginning to shun marriage and were opting for important careers. But I met and married a wonderful man, and we settled in Kansas. I continued to attend college classes and studied in Mexico on a full scholarship, where I looked for and purchased all sorts of fiber art and needlework, all the while collecting crochet patterns and yarn. Crochet had become my creative outlet for its sheer portability. When my new husband, Larry, and I purchased our first home, I began to crochet incessantly. I made sweaters, scarves, slippers, pillows, and all sorts of small items that would work up quickly. I had very little time, but crochet became an obsession. Yet within three years, not surprisingly, life interrupted once again by the delivery of another angel, Gabriel, Michael's new brother.

My language skills and minority studies proved to be important for the long term, as during my seventh month of pregnancy with Gabriel, on our third wedding anniversary, I slipped on ice chips that had been spread out on the floor of the variety store where we stopped for a small item. When I hit the wet and slick ice, my full weight landed on my left wrist, causing it to twist unnaturally. I wound up with what looked like a Z instead of an arm. It took two painful reductions and eight months of physical

Hooked

and occupational therapy before I had so much as the use of a finger on my left hand. The nursing career I was working toward was deemed finished.

Gabriel was born prematurely and became ill. When we finally brought him home, he required feeding every two hours around the clock. He had no sucking reflex, so I filled preemie bottles with my pumped milk and then tried to teach him to suckle afterward. He eventually caught on, but ate very slowly. During Gabriel's first four months of life, I crocheted four alphabet pillows for my brother's children. The pillows were made of three-inch granny squares that had to be sewn together in the shape of the particular letter of each of their names and then stuffed. While nursing the baby, I learned to use my broken arm in its cast as an anchor for the yarn. I wrapped the yarn around one of my useless left fingers with my right hand and crocheted the squares.

Eventually I finished a liberal-arts degree. I went on to graduate school and earned a masters of arts in liberal studies-Latin America. As an undergraduate, I had traveled to the Soviet Union, where I encountered many Latin Americans and found my ability to communicate in Spanish very helpful. The experience piqued my curiosity in Latin American affairs and lead me toward my graduate work.

A Life With Crochet

Eventually I became known for my interest and expertise in Latin American issues.

These days, all of my close friends think of me as much a crocheter as much any other label they might attach to me, including "always busy." For years I had taken on a variety of roles in order to fulfill my life and take care of my family. I traveled to Central America and other places as part of my studies and work, and, after I had spent a summer as an intern looking for and interviewing migrant workers for the California State Board of Education, my family and I moved back to California to live in the Sierra Nevada. I taught at the University and worked as the admitting coordinator/discharge planner and social services designee in a hospital.

In 1991, my husband received a telephone call from the vice president of the company he had worked for in Kansas. They needed him back and offered him an opportunity that was too good to refuse. Since we still owned our home in Wichita, we left the Sierra Nevada and moved back to our old house. I worked as a volunteer and education coordinator for a shop that sold arts and crafts, including crocheted items, made by fair-trade cooperatives around the world. Eventually, I became the program director of a truancy program that focused on the growing

Hooked

Hispanic community in our area. Sadly, I only managed to stitch for myself around the edges. But between various jobs, I did manage to crochet several items that brought the bliss of the creative process to me and the warmth and beauty of crochet to our home, even to our new, very large backyard.

After we'd returned to Kansas, my mother, who was still living in the mountains, fell and broke her pelvis. Shortly after, in 1992, we purchased a two-home compound. My mother moved into one house, and we got the Tudor cottage. I was inspired to decorate the new home with crochet. From the grape arbor covering our patio, I took vines and wound them into a distorted figure eight. Using every available pattern I could find, I crocheted a bouquet of a wide variety of flowers in as many colors and glued them around the grapevine wreath. I then embellished them with crocheted leaves and twisted copper wire. The wreath looked quite stunning on our front door. I crocheted one of Annie Potter's wreath designs with Irish roses and a very real looking bunch of grapes to adorn the stone wall over the fireplace. Using nylon cord, I stitched a trellis's worth of beaded squares to decorate an empty wall in the garden. Not all that surprisingly, my mother began to crochet again, as well. She graced us with gifts of doilies, crocheted dishcloths, and towel sets with crocheted edgings.

It was through the fall 1995 issue of *Piecework Magazine* that I learned a crochet guild had been founded. Thrilled, I joined immediately, and that summer I attended the Crochet Guild of America (CGOA) conference in Irvine, California. My first class was with the incredibly creative team of Sylvia Cosh and James Walters of Great Britain, who together made free-form crochet the art form it is today. I was both ecstatic and terribly nervous to be there. My experience in crochet was limited and never formal, and I knew that I had much to learn. Sylvia and James turned to nature as source for their work, and I found that awe inspiring. In creating their artwork with crochet, the team drew inspiration from Italian tiles, seashells, and stones, and they dyed yarns to match what they saw in nature. In the classroom, they displayed landscape-themed crocheted coats that they had made during the 1970s. Their art was not gaudy but soulful. Taking a class with Sylvia and James was incredible, although, to my chagrin, I have never found the time to complete free-form crochet projects of the kind I saw displayed during that workshop.

I remained busy with work during those years and in my spare time I attended Gabriel's soccer games and saxophone performances during his high school and early college years, which sometimes took him around the country. During these years, I wanted to do more complicated crochet, but muscle and nerve problems and a lack of spare time restricted me to more portable and simple projects. I did find a way to express my joy in crochet by doing something else—by writing occasional articles for the guild newsletter, *Chain Link*.

Interviewing and getting to know interesting crocheters has been one of the most rewarding experiences of my life. Beginning in 1996 and over the course of years, I have interviewed some very talented and well-known crocheters, including Carol Ventura, Annie Potter, Kate Coburn, Mary Buse Melick, and Gwen Blakley Kinsler, founder of the CGOA. I've written book reviews and editorials for *Chain Link*. Excerpts of two articles were published in the American Needlecraft Association newsletter, *The American Needlecrafter*. In 2004, my first article was published in the crochet magazine *Crochet Fantasy*. In the piece I profiled the creative, inventive master of color and crochet artisan Melody MacDuffee, who is known for her overlay crochet. After years of taking classes through the CGOA conferences and finally giving up the notion that I must work an eight to five o'clock workday, I found time and had my first designs published in *Crochet World* in the fall of 2004. I continue to write and design for magazines.

The perfect combination of travel opportunities and crochet came to my door via the guild as well. In 2000, I went to Ireland, England, and Wales as part of the first CGOA Irish Crochet Tour. There I became reacquainted with Máire Treanor, author of *Clones Lace: The Story and Patterns of an Irish Crochet*, whom I had met at a conference. I eventually wrote an article about Máire for *Crochet Fantasy* magazine. In an article I wrote about Nancy Nehring, I included photos I had taken of crochet garments reminiscent of styles from the 1960s; both Nancy and I had marveled over these in a Cardiff, Wales, dress shop on that same trip. When Carol Ventura invited me to visit her while she taught tapestry crochet at the University of Guanajuato in Mexico in 2001, it would have taken death itself to stop me. One of the unexpected treats of that experience was to have arrived on March 8, International Women's Day. In the town plaza, women were gathered to celebrate the day and to provide information on a variety of topics. Among the many booths were women crocheting and selling their work. Both Carol and I found ourselves rapidly going from one booth to the next to find treasures made in crochet.

Hooked

In 2000, after I went to Ireland, the local paper published an article about me and the trip. Soon after, I founded the local chapter of the CGOA. Crochet has become an addiction for me. The repetitive motion of crochet is meditative, healing, and relaxing. I do it when I am happy; I do it when I am sad, lonely, depressed, thrilled, tired, and invigorated. And I do it nearly every place I go. Crochet is a double blessing in that it is something I give and something I get back through the sheer act of doing. While nerve damage forces me to take many breaks while crocheting, every day in which I am able to crochet, I find contentment and a universal sense of belonging.

Last winter, my close friend and stepmother-in-law, June, had a stroke and died. A coverlet that I had designed to June's specifications and color choices was draped over an antique wooden screen in my in-laws' living room. June had proudly showed it to friends and family. But it was when we were sorting through her belongings that I found an afghan I had made her as a gift while I was recovering from major surgery myself and still living in the Sierra Nevada. It was just a gigantic granny square, but it included every leftover scrap piece of yarn I owned at the time. Spreading the colors clear across our living room carpet, I put the odd mixture of colors together as appropriately as possible. June often used that afghan to wrap herself up in on cold winter nights or to lightly cover herself with during an afternoon nap. Now every time I see that funky, bold, and strangely colored throw, I think of her and our mountain home with the crocheted, Southwestern-hued curtains and the mountain views. June and I were from very different generations and places, but we met in the middle. It warms my heart to know that crochet was not only a frequent topic of discussion for us, but it also provided me a skill with which to make her a gift that she was able to use for many years. I realize that like my grandmother, mother, and sister, I, too, am building up a stash of crochet to leave behind to others.